SURVIVING
A STARTUP

Published by Endeavor Literary Press
P.O. Box 49272
Colorado Springs, Colorado 80949
www.endeavorliterary.com

ISBN Print Version: 978-1-7358671-2-0
ISBN Ebook: 978-1-7358671-3-7

Cover Design: James Clarke (jclarke.net), United Kingdom

Contents

SURVIVING A STARTUP

By Joel Houston

Foreword

Building a business is a story of firsts.

I got my first chance to help build a business over forty years ago. When my boss explained the opportunity, I thought I would be in charge of a palace of a warehouse while crossdocking a hundred containers of freight per week. I thought I would be responsible for operations and sales, and that I would be the face of the company at one of our most important hubs. I imagined having a nice office in a converted garage attached to the warehouse. I dreamed of fishing, hunting, and other outdoor opportunities that would be afforded by my move. I thought that the company would ship all my personal effects to my new home, including my car, and that I'd live happily ever after.

In reality, my "palace" was three thousand square feet of warehouse with four doors. To call it "a little small" would be like saying the pope is a little Catholic. My office space in the converted garage had no insulation, even though the temperatures in the city regularly dropped below zero Celsius in the winter. When it rained, the roof leaked. One of my clerks had to support an umbrella while she worked to keep water from landing on papcrwork.

The only truth to what my boss told me was that I would have to deconsolidate and deliver a hundred containers of freight per week.

As is typical with startups, there was no money for

improvements. So, I had to improvise. First, I placed concrete pilings in front of one warehouse door and then set up a forty-foot long by eight-foot wide barge whale deck on the pilings. That adaptation gave us access to a deck that could accommodate an additional eight containers. However, on snowy days we had to shovel and sweep that area clear so that the forklifts could operate outside. It was often akin to sweeping an ice rink, but we made it work.

On the below-zero days, everyone worked in shifts: fifteen minutes outside and fifteen minutes warming up inside. One time I was out there too long. The warehouse staff found me wandering around lost in the yard with no idea where or who I was.

To solve the office space situation, I gave some free freight deliveries to a customer in exchange for a twenty-foot container. I cut a hole in the warehouse wall and attached the container to it. Then I put three desks in there, one for me and two for the clerks. It wasn't much warmer than the garage, but it was a hell of a lot drier. As the business grew, I finally built a larger office inside the warehouse to fit seven people. There was no room or money for nice desks. Instead, I acquired some long kitchen counters and file cabinets and set the counters on the filing cabinets up against the wall. I built the walls and did the electrical work myself. Everything from the acoustic tiles to the flooring I got via trade.

For the next expansion, we opened the garage door at the far end of the warehouse and built a thirty-foot by eighty-foot pad of poured concrete and rebar that could accommodate many more trucks. I traded freight moves for materials. A buddy and I did all the manual labor, except that I traded freight services to have someone put a roof over the pad.

In all these adjustments, I had no master plan. I was making everything up as I went along. Each step was a first, but each improvisational project added to the whole of a successful company.

Improvisation is part of running most startups. A friend who owned a restaurant wanted to install a commercial exhaust fan, but he didn't have the money to buy one. I knew another restaurant owner who had just replaced his fan and was planning to take the old one to the trash, even though it still worked. I grabbed it and spent the weekend installing the fan in my friend's restaurant kitchen while trying to not fall off the pitched roof (alcohol might have made that riskier). I'd never done anything like that before, but I helped to improve my buddy's restaurant and life. Most small business owners are masters of improvisation. Every experience is unique.

After starting a few other businesses, I had the chance to partner with Joel and build our own warehousing company, another first in forty years of working with freight. Joel and I had worked together before. I knew him well. So, when the opportunity to start a business together came along, my answer was an automatic yes.

In *Surviving a Startup*, Joel has managed to capture the highs and lows of running our warehouse. His sense of humor and keen eye for detail make reading the book feel like it all happened yesterday, even though years have passed. The book offers many helpful ideas and "survival tactics" for aspiring entrepreneurs who are interested in starting a small company or trying to successfully run one. There are lessons to be found in every story, in every customer interaction, and in every pallet moved.

The "firsts" described in this book aren't fiction. This is the story that we lived. It proved to be a hell of a ride—one that I would not have missed. Having our shared stories memorialized in this book is something I will always cherish.

Chester, March 2022

Prologue:
A Cautionary Tale

I met Rick, who owned a cannery, through mutual acquaintances when I was starting up Joel's Warehouse. Upon entering his office, it was clear that the cannery had seen better days. The central heating and cooling systems had broken years ago. To keep his office warm on cold December days he plugged in a space heater. He mounted an air conditioner in his window to keep his office cool in the summer. The desks in his office were from the 1960s, and the computers were from the early 2000s. Everything was past its prime, but still functioning—including Rick.

During that first meeting at the cannery, there was a steady stream of activity in the offices around us: phone calls, papers shuffling, and people filing in and out. Every time the door separating the offices from the operation opened, the noise from the machines would crescendo.

I took note of the surroundings, but I did not assume that Rick lacked the ability to pay his bills or otherwise be a good customer. Based on my experiences with all types of people over many years, the physical conditions of businesses rarely indicated their financial health. That included brokers with offices in high-rise buildings. I had met people who looked successful but were struggling. I once met a guy with a dirty, old workspace like Rick's who had tens of millions of dollars in the bank, and who owned dozens of warehouses and hundreds of trailers. He had earned his money from a lifetime of demanding work and constant travel. That guy was in his fifties and never had time for a wife. Although he regretted that fact, his business was his lover, mistress, and wife.

At the time, I didn't know if Rick was just cheap (thrifty, in some eyes) or if he was struggling financially. He seemed to be unaware of how his offices might leave a negative impression on visitors, but I approached the meeting without any preconceived ideas.

It didn't take long in our conversation to realize that our business needs did not align. Then Rick asked me to share my backstory. I gave him a quick overview of Joel's Warehouse and described how we were trying to establish ourselves. Something about my story clicked with Rick, and for the next hour or so he related his woeful tale.

Rick was seventy-years old and wanted to retire. For the previous thirty years, he had been the owner of this hundred-year-old fish processing operation. Now the business was in trouble. He could have declared bankruptcy and ended his troubles, but he did not want that to be his legacy. He wanted to pay off his debts and close the company on his terms, not the terms of a bankruptcy court.

It had not always been like this for Rick. When he took

control of the company more than thirty years earlier, he had four canneries spread across two states. "We used to be one of the largest trucking companies in the state," Rick boasted. "We had over a hundred drivers under our flag to handle the export and distribution of the canned seafood." (Others I talked with later confirmed that claim, adding that he had been a real force in the trucking industry.) Then Rick leaned toward me and said, "Do you know how many drivers I have now?"

I shook my head.

"One," he said, with a little anger in his voice. "And I don't know that I can even keep him for much longer."

The ports had imposed increasingly strict emissions standards on trucks entering and leaving ocean terminals, putting older trucks out to pasture. Engines had to be built no earlier than 2007. Rick's driver was running a truck built in the 1990s, and Rick could not afford to lease or buy a newer truck. He also could not afford to hire truckers outside his company to deliver his canned goods to port.

Rick's problems had been accumulating for decades. His truck drivers and his cannery employees were unionized, and he had stopped making pension payments into the union plan years before. This did not affect retired employees; the union still paid their pensions in full. However, the union had been tracking Rick's account. The total amount he owed was six figures.

Rick went on to explain how difficult it had been to adapt to constant changes in his industry, regulatory and otherwise. His earlier successes had been based on the size and variety of the fishermen's catch in the Gulf of Alaska. But more recently, in some years, there had not been enough fish coming in to keep him busy, and several new competitors had eroded his market share.

Rick tried to adjust by reducing his operation. He sold one of his canneries in another state. He ultimately closed the other two local canneries and eliminated drivers. He was able to narrow his operation down to one cannery, enabling him to operate successfully for a dozen years.

"The industry hit a low point a couple of years ago," said Rick sadly. "We went weeks at a time without a production run. I could not pay any of my bills. My landlord was pissed at me, and the union was all over me. I have not taken a paycheck in years and I'm behind on paying some of my managers. I don't know what I'm going to do."

Given that I was just starting my own business, Rick's troubles stung me to my core. I knew I was taking a risk when I opened Joel's Warehouse, but I had never heard such a deep-in-the-shit story from someone like Rick. He was clearly in over his head, and he needed more than a snorkel to keep breathing. He needed a ladder, or a rope, or someone who could pull him out. I was not that person. All I could do was to listen.

I occasionally checked up on Rick, each time hoping to hear a happy outcome. Less than a year later, there was a happy ending of sorts. Rick found another canning company that was willing to take over his operation (but not his debts). Rick would receive a monthly stipend based on the ongoing business from his existing customer base.

To get things back on track, the new owners of the cannery went directly to all of Rick's customers and increased their rates, significantly. As a result, some customers decided to get bids from other suppliers. They soon found out that Rick had been charging them much less than market rates for years. In no time, every customer accepted the new rate increase and stayed on with the canning company.

"I had no idea," Rick told me. It sounded like he might cry. My heart broke for him. He realized how much money he had lost over the years. Had he raised his rates earlier, it would have changed his life and the fortunes of his company.

The new owners of Rick's canning company also had a diversified portfolio. They had other product lines. If canning seafood suffered a down year, then lentils, poultry, and vegetables could pick up the slack. Rick, on the other hand, had never diversified. He had been good at canning seafood, and that's what he did to the end.

As Rick transitioned out of his long-held business, the cannery's landlord forgave him for falling behind on the building lease. The new canning company was financially stable and so the landlord was thrilled to have them assume control of the building. This stroke of luck probably spared Rick from paying tens of thousands of dollars in debt.

However, in a bittersweet moment, Rick had to sell a vacation house in a small oceanside community three hours from his home. It had been in his family for several generations, but he needed the money badly to pay some debts. Rick first used money from the house sale to pay the managers whose paychecks had been shorted. They had all been retained by the new canning company, and now they each got payments from Rick to make up for the hard times.

The last time Rick and I talked, he was enjoying retirement but still trying to resolve some debts. I admired him for his brave approach to his troubles. He didn't run and hide from his debts or seek relief via bankruptcy like many people would have. Rick handled his challenges with grace and did everything he could to set things right . . . at great cost to himself.

Rick's story is a cautionary tale. I do not mean that in a judgmental way. It might be easy to list—after the fact— what he could have done differently to help his business survive: charge his customers more; diversify the canning or trucking operation; adapt better to the changing regulatory environment and markets. Maybe. But none of us were in Rick's seat when he made his decisions. In fact, his company might have died much earlier without Rick's stewardship. Or maybe he just ran into a bit of bad luck.

Perhaps Rick knew what to do but lacked the capacity to implement the solutions. For example, imagine that the wood front porch of your house had rotted and fallen apart. You lack money to hire a contractor, and you do not have the skills to build the new porch yourself. You know you have a problem, but you can't address it. Instead, you start walking around the house and entering through the sliding door on the back patio. It is the best you can do until you save up enough money to replace the porch. However, that leads to another problem. The sliding door can't be locked or unlocked from the outside. So, when no one's home, you leave it unsecured. One unlucky day, while you are at work, you get robbed. Your problems have now multiplied because your TV has been stolen. You're doing the best you can, but many people conclude that you're an idiot.

That's why I don't judge Rick.

Rick's story should be a warning for business owners and for those who aspire to start up a business. Success can be fleeting. We cannot control or know everything. We can only control how we react to hardships and how we fight through them. We can hope that good times will last forever, but if they don't, we can handle the adversity with strength, kindness, and conviction—like Rick.

Or we could turn to alcohol, drugs, and sex . . . Hopefully, this book will help you avoid those vices, because they'll only make matters worse. And there are other reasons for reading the book. It will provide new and aspiring entrepreneurs an inside look at what it takes to run a business in non-technology sectors. Although tech startups are sexy these days, the vast majority of American business owners operate small firms—bookstores, construction companies, wine shops, plumbing and HVAC services, canneries, and . . . warehouses. Companies like these are often overlooked, but they keep the world running. The supply chain problems in 2021 have demonstrated that the world stops without trucking companies, port workers, and others who are often overlooked in our society.

So, unlike many business books written by suited guys with MBAs and white teeth, this book is an in-the-trenches survival guide for starting and sustaining a business. It is a memoir written by someone who learned in the "school of hard knocks," a person who learned through experience not theory.

The true events in this book happened years ago and my memory is not perfect. Thus, the conversations presented are accurate in substance, but they are not verbatim. I did not carry a tape recorder around with me.

During my daily commutes to and from Joel's Warehouse, I sometimes imagined myself as the Tony Soprano of warehousing. That habit will account for some of the hyperbole in the book. Take those references with a grain of salt.

In summary, this book is a raw look at the trials and triumphs of running a small business. If you already own one, you'll find some tips and strategies from a fellow business owner. If you're thinking about starting a business, you'll get a crash course on dealing with licenses, government, taxes, suppliers, and customers. If you're just curious, you'll get an uncensored view of a small business owner's life, conveyed with the humor that's helped me survive life's challenges.

As always, keep surviving!

1

Taking the Leap

There are a thousand reasons to take the leap and start your own business.

Perhaps, at your current company, you landed a multimillion-dollar account. It took you six months of working long hours. You traveled enough to add five hundred thousand miles to your rewards card. You missed your baby's first steps, gained fifteen pounds from eating out all the time, and caught something from that nice gal or guy in Detroit with questionable hygiene and flexible morals.

Then, after the contract was signed, your employer made a big deal about the new account with a company-wide announcement. Your boss gave you the impression that you would get a nice bonus, a promotion, and pay raise. But a week later, it all evaporated. Your boss immediately started to hound you to make the next big sale. And you wonder, *Why am I working so hard so that someone else can make the money?*

Perhaps you are like Microsoft employee Jim Lane who, according to a 2008 article in the *Mirror,* left in 1985 after years of sweat and toil because the company "had beat the enthusiasm out of me." Although he missed the massive growth of Microsoft in the nineties, Jim founded his own companies and ended up with an estimated net worth of $39 million. If you ever want to know how to make lemons into lemonade, Jim seems like a good guy to ask.

Regardless of your reasons for taking the leap, the first step is to understand your comfort level with risk.

Fear and Risk

Unless you have money to burn, your biggest obstacle to starting a business will be fear. You realize that you could sink everything you have into the company, maybe even your house, and that the business could go belly up. If that happens, then all the times you teased your spouse that he or she should work nights "on the boulevard" to make extra money will no longer sound like jokes.

Fear emerges from the recognition of risk. So, to minimize fear you need to think about how to minimize risk. There are a lot of ways to do that. One is to get a partner. You could ask your spouse to go to work (not on the boulevard). You could start small. You could make sure your customer agreements are ironclad. Whatever the case, risk-minimization strategies always depend on the nature of each business.

The first step is to write down all the risks you can imagine and describe how you plan to minimize them. When I started Joel's Warehouse, I had to guarantee that I would pay the warehouse lease. At $13,000 per month, I knew I would go broke fast if the business had a problem. However, I had a partner in the venture. Chester chipped in a 40 percent stake.

That reduced my exposure to $7,800 per month, but it meant two families would go bankrupt and lose their houses if the business failed.

With Chester as a partner, the chances of success increased. For one, he guaranteed that I would have another worker show up every day. Chester also had skills that complemented mine, which proved to be essential for our eventual success. Part of me preferred to go it alone, but I knew I needed help to run a large warehouse.

Our greatest risk minimizer was a strong and stable customer who, on average, could provide us with $30,000 per month in revenue. We knew that would more than cover our $17,000 in monthly warehouse expenses, but we didn't know if there would be money left for us to collect a paycheck. My initial estimates indicated that we could make it work, but how would reality line up with my spreadsheet?

To be specific, we had to factor in the rental of two forklifts at $1000 per month. Insurance for the business, warehouse, and forklifts added another $1000 per month. We also needed an employee to run the forklift. We needed office supplies, computers, a payroll system, a website, business licenses (city and incorporation with the state), a propane supplier for operating the forklifts, a legal bill of lading, and a dozen other details. We also had to pay the first and last month's rent on the warehouse.

All of this meant coming up with $26,000 before we could do anything else. To minimize risk, we decided to seed the business with $50,000 out of our pockets rather than from a bank loan. It wasn't easy, but we managed it. It would take years for the company to pay us back for that initial loan, but it eventually did.

Perhaps most importantly, we had the right *attitude* and *experience* to reduce our risks. My partner had over forty years of experience in shipping, and I had fifteen years. I also had a wide variety of administrative skills, which helped us manage the business. We were confident in our ability to overcome obstacles, but fear lurked in our minds. As former Secretary of Defense Donald Rumsfeld warned, there are "unknown unknowns." We believed we could make everything work in theory, but we also knew that reality would be different than theory.

What is the point of developing a plan if theory doesn't match reality? At worst, a plan will ensure the office has sufficient toilet paper, or perhaps humorous reading material. In the best-case scenario, a plan will work as, well, planned. If so, you will feel like a genius—along the lines of Forrest Gump, not Stephen Hawking—but that's better than nothing.

Our plan produced a mixed bag of results. Sometimes the plan worked well, but we got caught with our pants down (metaphorically) numerous times. Regardless, I am sure that by developing a plan we minimized risk and increased our chances for success.

Best Laid Plans

The first day was easy. Supplies and a couple of forklifts arrived. Then we killed the lights. We had not done much, but we still felt good. We knew that on day two, the first containers would show up.

What we didn't know was that all our plans would go out the window. As soon as the first container arrived from the port, we realized that we did not have any bolt cutters, which we needed to open the steel seals used on international shipping containers. Chester and I were familiar with domestic shipping containers, which use plastic seals. Fortunately, the truck driver had a pair of bolt cutters in his truck, and he was able to open the container.

With the container doors open, we discovered that the dock plates built into the warehouse doors did not align with the height of over-the-road (OTR) trailers. By contrast, a shipping container on a chassis sits between four to eight inches higher than an OTR trailer. This vertical step up made it nearly impossible for our forklift to access the container. We had no idea what to do. Fortunately, people from the business next to ours were willing to loan us a solid steel dock plate, which they maneuvered into position by using their forklifts.

The freight inside was double-stacked bags of plastic resin. With each "supersack" weighing approximately 2500 pounds, the total weight per pallet was more than five thousand pounds. Chester, driving the forklift, tried to remove the first double-stacked pallet out of the container. The top bag promptly fell off and landed upside down on the warehouse floor. No damage occurred to the product, but we had a 2500-pound bag of resin resting upside down on the floor. Each supersack had four handles designed to be lifted by the forks, but the handles on this one were now buried underneath the bag. With some maneuvering, we got the bag to slump over on its side. This enabled us to grab two handles with the forklift and then set the bag aright. It took us thirty minutes to remove the first pallet, and we had nine pallets left to unload. It was an inauspicious start.

Our sole employee, the legendary Mutt, jumped on the forklift and showed us how to clear a container in about twenty minutes. Mutt had never handled this sort of product before, but he knew how to run a forklift and juggle double-stacked, fragile freight. His familiarity with forklifting came from years of working for his family's beer distribution business. All told, Mutt had moved thousands of pallets of beer. With Mutt's help, we eventually unloaded seven containers into the warehouse: seventy pallets, or 140 bags, or 350,000 pounds of product. Still, that day reminded us that reality does not conform to theoretical plans. The ability to be flexible and creative in the face of problems kept us moving forward.

Be Flexible and Creative

Starting a business is different than trying to run a business. At an established company, procedures have been in place for years or decades. In other words, someone has already made the mistakes and learned from them.

We did not have that advantage at Joel's Warehouse. We handled freight that we had never seen before in a new (to us) building, in a market with which we had little experience. We would have to make our own mistakes, figure out how to resolve them, and hopefully not repeat them. We relied on being flexible, creative, and humble.

The opposite of humility is pride. Pride deludes business owners into thinking that they have the experience and knowledge to solve problems, when in fact they don't. Pride tells them that they do not need help or advice. Pride lures them into taking shortcuts that seem more efficient but cost heavily in the long run.

In humility, Chester and I asked the boys next door to our business for assistance with how to best use the warehouse space, and for help with the dock plate. If we had not asked them for help, it would have been tough for us to finish the first day much less receive the first twenty-five containers during the next two days.

After that job, we had a two-week breather, which we used to order two custom-built dock plates and various supplies. We also spent a lot of time talking to people, including folks who had previously handled those supersacks. We also experimented with how to store them. We decided we could stack them in a pyramid, which would allow us to store 30 percent more product in the same area. In the warehousing business, space is money. By creating as much room as possible, we were better able to grow our business. And when the second round of containers arrived at the port, we were better prepared.

During these first days and weeks of our startup, I saw that open communication and a willingness to listen had put us on a quick path to competency. Chester and I could not generate all the ideas on our own, but we were able to discern which ideas were bad and which were good. We applied the good ones, regardless of who came up with them. We also gave proper credit to the person who came up with the solution.

Humility Leads to Teamwork

It takes humble leaders to build a strong team and business culture. Thus, humility means that when things go well, the credit belongs to everyone else, and when things go poorly, all the blame belongs on the business owner. If that sounds unfair, then prepare to "suck it up, buttercup," as Chester often said. For us, if an employee made a mistake on paperwork or handled the freight wrong, it was a training issue. When our first employee, Mutt, peed off the dock (more on that later), then we were responsible for correcting the behavioral issue, even though Mutt was in his seventies at the time. In that case, I delegated the behavioral issue to Chester, because he and Mutt had been friends for forty years.

"He's not housebroken," Chester explained to me. "He's like a dog, you just need to smack his nose with a newspaper every once in a while."

Shortly after, Mutt came roaring by on a forklift, barking at us the whole way.

"See?" Chester emphasized. "Not housebroken."

I never smacked Mutt with a newspaper, but I adjusted for

the fact that both Chester and Mutt were in their seventies. I know what you're thinking. *You mean this guy started a warehousing business with two septuagenarians?* It felt like the movie series *The Expendables.*

Despite their age and quirks, they were good at their work. When Mutt and Chester were both on the forklifts, I had more than eighty years of experience cruising through the warehouse. I was probably the only warehouse owner in the state, or perhaps in the country, with that level of bull riding experience.

Ultimately, we built the operation bit by bit by drawing on the experience of all three of us, our warehouse neighbors, friends, spouses, competitors, customers, and anyone else we could ask for help. As we grew, we showed new employees how we preferred to operate, but we invited staff to share creative ideas with us. Our success was owned by a lot of people, but the failures were all mine. I'm comfortable with that. To own a business means owning all of it—even the cleanliness of the toilets, or lack thereof.

To optimize the chances of success, the members on the team should complement each other. The strengths of one should support the weaknesses of another. I wanted to work with people who had strengths to cover for my weaknesses. I'll write more about this later, but I learned that I needed to know myself as a leader before I could find people to compensate for my skill gaps.

Chester and I had been friends for many years. Thirty years my senior, he was first a customer, then a mentor, then an employee, then a business partner, and always a friend.

Because I knew him so well, I could see that his skills complemented mine. For example, I knew how to design a website, handle the financials, create contracts and bills of lading, incorporate the business, manage our IT needs, handle vendors, talk to customers, dispatch trucks, and keep the operation organized. Chester shared some of my skills, but he also knew how to build crates, unload vehicles, chain freight, pull freight, push freight, lift freight, and talk to anyone anywhere anytime. He also enjoyed whipping employees, truck drivers, and customers into shape.

Mutt had been Chester's friend for at least forty years. As mentioned earlier, he had a lengthy career in freight handling. His ties to the local community were strong, perhaps developed by his habit of playing five rounds of golf every week. Mutt could talk the ears off a mule while zipping around on a forklift.

We each had our strengths and weaknesses, but as a team we were able to prop each other up. During those years, I learned that the best teams have diverse skills and approaches to problem solving. Diversity allows the team to handle more tasks, catch more mistakes, and create more solutions. The downside is the risk of driving each other crazy. Chester and I certainly had our moments of tension, but we had the same goal of creating a successful business that could support our families. We questioned each other, but not our motives. Some tension helped us to be successful.

The best ideas are haggled out, tested, debated. In this way, they either survive the gauntlet of doubt or fall aside. When I saw a plan or idea that had not been debated or challenged, I immediately doubted its efficacy. Even existing plans needed to be continually tested against new ideas. If a current procedure stood up against the new ideas, then great. If not, then I would change it. Team collaboration requires company leaders to be willing to change long-established procedures. Doing so communicates that the leaders are open to the team's ideas.

I once worked for a company that only shipped freight using forty-foot containers. The president/owner of the company had spent his entire thirty-year career using that size of equipment. Other employees had failed to convince him to change. After I was hired, it took me six months to help him to branch out. Over the next couple of years, we bought hundreds of pieces of equipment, ranging from twenty-foot containers to fifty-three-foot trailers. Our profits rose as we fit the container to the freight, rather than making all freight fit a forty-foot container.

Chester and I learned a key lesson about running a startup: avoid a yes-man business culture. This might not be easy, but a yes-man culture will stifle creativity. It requires a certain type of leader and attitude to give team members freedom to express their views, and not be expected to pander to the boss. Without that type of culture, employees will often hide problems rather than look for solutions.

I encourage you to surround yourself with people who will not "mirror" you, but rather with people who will complement you. Diversity of thought can lead to innovative ideas as the company faces new challenges.

2

Leadership

As the head of your own business, people will look to you to set the tone for behavior and achievement. But no one is a born leader who never needs to learn. Rather, leadership requires study and practice. To grow in leadership skills, we need advice from mentors. Only then will we be able to execute well. The alternative would be like asking a seven-year-old who has never had piano lessons to play Mozart.

How do you get started on a journey to be a more effective leader? Is the time and effort going to really make a difference? How much is it going to cost? I don't know what your journey is going to look like, but perhaps you can learn something from mine.

Learn What to Do

I have had about a dozen direct bosses over the years, with perhaps another two dozen indirect bosses with whom I interacted regularly. These people included managers, the boss's boss, and peers who influenced my career. I often had to report my progress on projects to at least six different people, each with their leadership styles and their own demands.

The bad part of that arrangement is obvious. Two of them (my manager and my manager's manager) might have been able to directly influence my paycheck, whereas the others could exert influence on my direct managers if they felt I was not performing. It was always a careful juggling act to keep everyone happy. People love to gossip, so I assumed that anything I did or said in a meeting might find its way back to my boss.

On the bright side, I gained great exposure to many aspects of the company and to projects that most employees did not get to see. I was also able to interact with senior managers and vice presidents who taught me about leadership. Most were willing to give me time and share their insights, and I was eager to observe and listen.

For example, there was a CEO who made it a point to remember the staff members' alma maters. Even years later, he brought up some sort of sports trivia or other factoid about the university where one of us attended. We were all shocked that he could remember so much. This was the CEO's way to be personal with each employee. I learned a lot from that leader!

Today, I often seek to learn and remember something about each person I work with for future reference. I sometimes add notes to my cellphone contact cards so that I can refer to that information later. For example, I learned that one customer preferred a certain type of Kentucky bourbon, so I delivered a bottle at Christmas. I often memorize the names of my colleagues' family members if they share that information.

In future conversations, I mention specific names rather than just generically saying, "How's the family?"

Those who are a bit cynical might see these efforts as "tricks" meant for leaders to win the good graces of other people. But if those cynics approach relationships in a cynical way, the cynicism will show through. Instead, they should consider how much effort it takes to be more personal in work situations, and to remember that expending effort is a sign of caring.

Early in my career, a manager told me that she never received compliments "because no one ever thinks to compliment the boss. Sometimes I wish someone would tell me that I did a good job." I've made it a point since then to compliment people when it seemed appropriate and natural, including my bosses. This is a fine line to walk because no one wants you to blow smoke up their ass, but there are plenty of legitimate reasons to encourage people.

The best way to compliment someone is to stay away from generic statements, such as, "You're doing a good job," and to be specific, such as, "Good job talking to that driver about how he wanted his trailer loaded." This approach also helps people understand which behaviors you want them to emulate. Perhaps your staff will focus on those things and avoid negative behaviors, such as, "Chester, don't call every French-Canadian you see a dirty frog." (More on that later).

While I was working at Joel's Warehouse, a former boss paid me a visit. He had started up a competing warehouse about five miles away. He only stayed at my site for a few minutes, but I saw his eyes darting here and there as we walked through my warehouse. I got the impression that he was trying to identify my customers. He noticed that we had a lot of business and commented, "Chester has always been good at sales." Then he departed, in a hurry. I was a little surprised and disappointed.

My gut feeling was that his new warehouse wasn't doing very well, and he needed help. I also got the impression that he didn't want to ask me for help directly but decided to spy on me instead. If so, his assumptions were ridiculous. If he had asked, I would have given him some leads on business that we couldn't handle. We were bursting at the seams. As a leader, I'm in favor of trying to help other businesses when possible. Competition is part of business, but we can still be good human beings.

One of the vice presidents I worked for had once owned his own company. After selling it, he took a couple of years off. He wrote down some behaviors that, in his view, characterized good leaders. He carried that notecard with him as a reminder to emulate those behaviors. When he took over as vice president of the department in which I worked, he became a mentor. He also served as a source of quotes that I still use, including this one: "With your bosses, sometimes you learn what to do, and sometimes you learn what not to do."

Learn What Not to Do

Every interaction with leaders in your company can be a chance to learn about leadership, but sometimes they don't display the behaviors you should emulate. For example, the same vice president who gave me good quotes had the annoying habit of letting the employees his age propose ideas without adequately justifying them. In contrast, he would not sign off on proposals from younger employees unless we provided thirty pages of statistics to back up them up.

In one such instance, I shared an opinion that directly contradicted one of the vice president's older cronies. The vice president sided with his peer and told me I would need to provide data to change his mind. Later I approached the vice president and pointed out how older staff were being treated differently than younger staff, and that it was always incumbent on younger workers to provide all the analysis. I suggested that older workers should also need to justify their ideas.

To his credit, he agreed that he had treated younger employees differently. He then promised to monitor his approach and try to be fairer when listening to contradictory opinions. But by the time I left the company, my relationship with the vice president, which had been strong for years, had completely deteriorated. He was the reason I left. Studies, such as a 2017 LinkedIn survey, consistently show that 75 percent of employees who have resigned from a job did so because of struggles with a manager. This indicates how important it is to learn and practice good leadership skills. Otherwise, companies will be more likely to struggle with high employee turnover.

Two months later I saw that vice president again at an industry event. I shook his hand and thanked him for his willingness to invest in my career for so many years. His parting words were, "You'll find all this was just a small blip in your life and didn't mean much in the grand scheme of things. Just keep pressing on." We have not spoken since, but I still think of him frequently and fondly. I decided to not let our relationship be defined by the last few bad months. I learned a lot from him, and his parting words were full of wisdom.

My first professional job was with an airfreight company that went through a multibillion-dollar merger within the first few years of my employment. As an employee at the corporate office, my two options were to take a generous severance package or move to the new corporate office on the other side of the country. I chose the severance package, but they gave me about a year of advance notice about when the job would end.

That left plenty of time for job hunting. Everyone in my department who chose not to move across the country started hitting the streets. I would say that approximately 90 percent of the people in the department were looking for a new job, including most of the managers.

After a job interview for an analyst position with another airfreight company, I returned to work. My manager asked a bunch of questions about the company, the job, and the hiring manager. I answered the questions honestly and then forgot about it until the following week. That's when my manager announced that she had a new job with the company where I had just interviewed.

As I subsequently found out, my manager had taken the information I gave her and spoke to the hiring manager. They interviewed her for the same position that I had applied for. They raised the job level from an analyst position to a management position and offered her the job.

I have no idea what my odds were for getting the analyst job. I do know that my odds went to zero after my manager got the job. It would be another ten months before I got an acceptable offer for a similar position in a related industry.

As you learn "what not to do," your experiences could make you jaded. I'm naturally a transparent person with nothing to hide. My hobbies—video games, bass fishing, and Legos—are probably the most interesting things about me. I also love my family and have a few anecdotes about my kids. In short, I'm boring.

I could have been much less transparent after I experienced the pain of a manager taking my job opportunity. I could have become more secretive and evasive. I probably could have become bitter. The experience could have changed me in negative ways. But I decided not to let that happen. Why? Because the one thing I have control over is how I respond to being burned.

In retrospect, a great thing happened as a result of not getting that analyst position. I ended up meeting Katie, who is now my wife, at my next job with the ocean shipping line. What I have now is great, and I wouldn't trade it for anything.

But the main leadership lesson I learned from being burned by my former manager was: Don't ever be that type of person.

In what ways you can build a leadership toolbox? For me, the quickest and most effective way to learn is by reading.

A Good Book

Successful leaders have a lifelong love of learning. I love books, preferably physical copies that I can hold in my hands and reread days, months, or years later. Some books can change your life.

The catalyst for an evolutionary period in my life is a well-known book called *Seven Habits of Highly Successful People*. One of the companies I worked for emphasized ongoing training and leadership classes, some of which involved a study of this book. At first, I was skeptical about *Seven Habits*, but the company wanted me to attend a three-day class with content based on the book. I was only a senior analyst at the time, so I reasoned that getting my face out there among other company leaders would be good for my career. I had already been involved in a variety of important projects, and they kept assigning me to the most difficult and high-profile stuff. I figured a promotion to management was not far off.

A coworker, who we will call Dan, was a fifteen-year veteran of the company when I showed up. He was also thirty years my senior. I had four years of experience as an analyst with a different company, and I had the energy and drive to change anything I considered outmoded or inefficient. I thought I was doing everyone a favor by putting my creativity to work. It did not take long for me to build positive relationships with everyone in the company. Unfortunately, I could not break through with Dan. We constantly found ourselves at loggerheads over reports, data querying, customer pricing, tariff language, and even how strong we preferred our coffee.

As Dan would tell me years later, "When you came in, it seemed like everything we ever did was wrong, and that you were going to fix it your way."

I never meant to make him feel that way, but looking back I can see why he would have that impression. I never considered how my approach might make others feel, especially a long-time employee like Dan. I never asked him what he thought about my suggestions. I simply assumed that my initiatives would speak for themselves.

By the time I took the *Seven Habits* class, my relationship with Dan had cemented into cordial but distant. The *Seven Habits* book includes many suggestions for building relationships. As part of the class, the instructor asked each of us to write briefly about a problematic relationship and a resolution to fix it.

I wrote down Dan's name. I knew he was a good guy and I saw no reason why we could not get along. I wanted to fix the relationship because it would be better for the department. I also wanted to grow as a person. If I could turn this relationship around, it would show *me* that I had the potential to do and be better.

I began to make several changes in my relationship with

Dan. I became more patient when he explained the way they "had always done things." I tried to understand the *what* and the *why,* and I made it clear that I had been listening to him. Instead of arguing about why my ideas were better, I explained my perspective and gave him a couple of days to consider suggestions. As it turned out, he became more receptive to my positions.

By listening, I gained more insight into the challenges that Dan faced in his work. I was able to help him solve some of his problems by giving him some ideas, helping him directly, or interceding with the IT department on his behalf. I was mostly successful with the IT folks. I suppose they found me to be just as energetic and annoying as Dan did. They found it easier to give me what I wanted than say no.

As months passed, Dan's attitude about me changed. He soon realized that I was an ally in his fight. I also made sure that Dan received the credit for the work. I cleared some roadblocks, but he was the one who got stuff done, not me. Dan grew to appreciate me even more when he realized that I was not out to steal the credit.

Thankfully, we worked things out. Less than a year later I was promoted and became his boss. After I left the company, Dan admitted to me that I had changed from being the "young guy fighting him every day" to "the best boss I ever had." I appreciated the feedback, especially knowing how much work I had put into our relationship.

I encourage you to spend regular time looking for good books on leadership, team building, and business. As a lifelong learner, you can always grow as a leader. Some of the books and resources that I recommend are shown below.

1. *The Speed of Trust* by Stephen M.R. Covey (Stephen R. Covey's son).
2. *The Program* written by two marines, Eric Kapitulik and Jake MacDonald. Their emphasis is on building high performing teams.
3. *Win or Die* by Bruce Craven provides leadership lessons from the popular HBO show "Game of Thrones."
4. *Skin in the Game* by Nassim Nicholas Taleb. This book tackles complicated matters of ethics and risk.
5. Myers-Briggs tests, or the similar 16personalities.com website. I recommend taking this test and having friends, employees, and coworkers take it. At minimum, the results should spark healthy discussions, but ideally the results will help you relate to others on your team.

As you learn from leadership books and mentors, be sure to maintain your own style. My style grew out of my experiences in large companies and as a small business owner. I learned a lot from my former bosses, but the books I read often reshaped my thinking and behaviors.

Shaping Your Leadership Style

I was once a hard charging know-it-all. Now I am an older, slower charging, and more strategic know-just-enough-to-get-into-trouble-and-sometimes-out-of-it type of guy. It took a series of revelations for me to understand what was good and bad about my approach. For example, I learned that it is great to have energy, especially when it comes to change. But it's also important to remember that many people are resistant to change. It is not a good idea to use that energy to make the change happen despite objections from peers and employees. We need those folks to help get stuff done.

As I launched Joel's Warehouse, realization number one was: I couldn't do it all. I had to shore up my weaknesses by relying on the team of folks around me. I had to trust people to support me and each other, to bolster each other's weaknesses. That was the only way we could pull in the same direction, like a team of dogs pulling a sled. Through trust and working together, we could make a lot more progress.

I also concluded that a department full of Joels would be a pain in the ass. I would much rather manage a department of Dans (quiet, effective workhorses) than a department of Joels (high energy, never satisfied). Ideally, I wanted a department full of variety, with maybe one Dan, one Mutt, one MP, one Chester, one Katie, and one Joel.

Dan and Mutt are the sort of guys who show up every day and contribute steadily without fanfare. Chester is the kind of guy who demands more from everyone: employees, vendors, and customers. MP is the type of person who takes his job personally. When things are not going well, he uses his anger to drive himself to work harder and overcome challenges. Katie is the type of person who can run on her own after she asks some questions. I am the type of guy who shows up and gets a lot done, but not without constantly pushing the envelope on current procedures, thought processes, and hierarchies.

In short, all leaders need teams with complementary—but not contradictory—skills. We need harmony with a little chaos. Complete harmony would be stagnation. We need to challenge each other, but we need to do it with respect while keeping an eye on the overall goals.

I also knew that to be a good leader, I needed to become a better listener. To motivate people, I needed to understand what motivated them. A boss who believes that people should be motivated "because I'm paying them" should probably reevaluate what it means to be a leader. To show up for work just to get paid is the minimum tradeoff. Motivation is not always tied to money.

When it comes to leading a startup, being a good listener is a key to survival. Without true listening, you will not be able to hear the promising ideas that come from others around you. When I say listen, I do not mean simple hearing. I mean listening to understand. This does not happen naturally. Most of us are actively preparing our responses while the other person is talking, which means that we are not actually listening. As a startup owner, you will have the authority to make big decisions. You will get the blame for failures while your employees get the credit for successes. So, make sure you have listened carefully before you make decisions.

Our success at Joel's Warehouse was tied to our ability to listen to each other, to our employees, and to vendors, customers, and competitors. Not everything we heard was helpful, but our patience often paid off.

In addition, I learned that being proactive, which is the first of the *Seven Habits,* does not mean charging forward immediately. Leaders should be self-motivated and proactive, but sometimes that energy can rub people the wrong way. I learned that lesson when I bulldozed my way through Dan's workspace.

My former mentor and vice president often said, "Sometimes, if you just sit on a problem for a day or two, it will resolve itself." That approach used to annoy me. It seemed to make more sense to address problems immediately and then move on.

As it turned out, my mentor was right. One downside of tackling a problem immediately is that there might be a better way to solve it. To find the best solution, it might take a day or two of thinking. Without patience, we can apply suboptimal solutions based on gut instinct or on previous experiences. Patience also gives other people who are close to the problem a chance to provide ideas that might make the resolution simpler.

I am not saying you should sit on every problem. If I added ketchup to a man's hamburger when he asked me to hold the ketchup, I do not need a committee to decide whether to get the man a new hamburger. But it is easy to fall into "paralysis by analysis" wherein leaders can't ever make a decision because everyone is perpetually reviewing the same options. Sometimes the solution to a problem is obvious and we need to act immediately. Wisdom could be described as knowing the difference.

Fourth, I learned to discern between helpful and unhelpful

criticism. A CEO once described me as having a "rhinoceros hide," referring to my attitude in the face of negative feedback. I believe my entire department at that company was equally thick-skinned. We were often the bearers of bad news, and we often had to make decisions that other departments didn't agree with. So, a lot of criticism came our way.

As the leader of your small business, you should be prepared for the slings and arrows. If you can, develop tough rhinoceros hide. You are going to need it. Customers might be unhappy. Employees might not like it if you ask them to work overtime. Vendors might not like your explanation for a late or short payment. Competitors won't appreciate it when you capture some of their business.

On the other hand, you should be open to helpful criticism. Doing so can avert disaster. You should not become so immune to criticism that you also become immune to learning. If you can't learn, you can't adapt. If you can't adapt, you're going to struggle.

Fifth, I learned to see that my role as a leader is to support others. People with whom you work will make the company successful, so you should provide the resources and support they need to be successful.

If someone in my warehouse needed a tool to do the job, I bought it. Did my staff need time to vent? I was all ears. Were they tied up with a difficult customer or struggling to collect from a late payer? I would assume responsibility for that customer so that my employee could move on to other work.

The key is, within reason, to make sure the employees

can be productive. I have always preferred to flip the typical organizational chart upside down. The workers whose daily transactions earn the company money shouldn't be carrying the burden of supporting all the managers above them. In my mind it should be the managers who support the folks in operations, so that those people can efficiently generate more revenue.

Finally, I have always tried to be congruent, to ensure that my words and actions reflect how I feel. We all know phony people. As Stephen Covey wrote in *Seven Habits*, "Who you are speaks so loudly I can't hear what you're saying." It does not matter what you say, if you don't believe it.

Leaders often say, "We're all in this together." Then you realize that the proposed change won't affect the leader much. That indicates a lack of congruence that will lead to distrust. Without trust, every interaction becomes more difficult, and everyone suffers.

These principles apply to business *and* to life. They are important in every relationship. Leadership is about relationships with other people. We should exercise these principles with our spouses, children, friends, and community.

In our marriage, Katie and I have a partnership. There are situations in which one of us takes the lead and the other one provides support. There is no "head of household" in the sense that one of us is in charge and the other one is always the follower. At the beginning of the Covid-19 lockdown, Katie took charge of the kid's online classes and homework for the end of the 2019-2020 school year. When they "returned" to a hybrid school situation for the fall 2020-2021 term, I took lead on their at-home education. Katie and I take turns helping each other keep the kids on track, but we defer to the parent who is the lead. We handle the household chores the same way. I'm in charge of paying the bills. Katie oversees laundry, in part because I don't have the time (or inclination) to read special care laundry instructions on labels. I cook most of the meals, but Katie sometimes makes dinner. I mow the lawn. Katie leads all holiday decorating activities.

To recap, good leaders:

- value complementary skills
- are good listeners
- are reasonably proactive
- have rhinoceros hide
- support others
- are congruent

Ultimately, you'll find out what works best for you. Keep learning, growing, and adapting. Write down what you want to work on and who you want to be. Then practice those skills and use them. It will pay dividends.

3

Customer Relations

I honed my understanding of business and customer relations when I worked for the ocean shipping company. When someone from finance complained about spending hundreds of thousands of dollars on fuel for one voyage, I suggested that we fire our customers. "Think of the fuel savings we could have if we never sailed the ships," I would say pointedly.

I had the same response for the vessel guys who complained about dirty ships. In fact, I said the same thing to everyone at work who complained about our clients, until no one in the entire company liked me anymore, except for my wife, and she resigned as soon as our oldest kid was born. That left exactly zero Joel fans at work.

At the warehouse, when the equipment guys would finish a repair job on a trailer that had been damaged by a customer, they often said something like, "We'll see how long before someone puts a forklift hole in the wall again."

"Let's fire the customers," I'd suggest. "Think of all the maintenance money we could save."

In my experience, salespeople are the only people who never complain about having customers, perhaps because they take them out for lunch and a round of golf every day on the company dime.

Here's my point: The only thing worse than having customers is not having customers. It's probably fair to say that my colleagues already knew that, but I have always been a master of the obvious.

One Customer

When we started the warehouse, we had one customer: Little Jimmy. As you can probably guess, having only one customer is exponentially worse than having many customers. It might even be worse than having no customers. Having one customer who pays all your bills means that your availability to that customer must be twenty-four hours a day, seven days a week, 365 days per year.

I could judge what sort of day I was going to have based on whether, first thing in the morning, Little Jimmy called to say, "I need your help." If Little Jimmy needed my help, it was guaranteed to cost me time, money, or both. It was my dream that one day he would call and tell me he had too much money and needed me to take some of it off his hands. Strangely, that never happened.

To summarize our relationship as all-take-and-no-give would be unfair to Little Jimmy. Like any meaningful relationship, we had our ups and downs. Our interactions were complex. I got to know him through a mutual friend, The Kid, who worked for me at a freight forwarding company with numerous warehouse locations. His role was to build a trucking arm for the company: buy tractors, hire employees, and add new customers.

Little Jimmy's main problem was that he had product spread across numerous warehousing companies. He wanted to simplify his life and unify his product under one roof, but none of his providers could handle it all. He also felt that his providers never gave him the level of service he needed. Little Jimmy needed his warehouse providers to offer flexible opening and closing hours, and not set strict appointment times. But the owners at large warehouse operations told him to either follow their schedules or find another company.

I presented Little Jimmy's volume, revenue, and service requirements to my boss, the owner of the freight forwarding company. Little Jimmy had some good business, but we realized that we would need to acquire another warehouse to accommodate his needs, which meant that we would also need more customers to make those new spaces profitable. So, my boss wanted us to focus on our core business. He had no interest in the distraction of setting up another warehouse. It also didn't help that Little Jimmy was part of the *international* shipping community. Our primary focus was on the markets regulated by the Jones Act, which pertains to US states and territories such as Guam, Hawaii, Puerto Rico, and Alaska.

I thought about it for a few days and discussed the opportunity with Chester, who was working at the same company as my director of pricing. It quickly became apparent that Chester and I wanted to pursue this opportunity together. It would be a departure from the freight world in which we had both cut our teeth, but it was also a much larger world, with big opportunities.

Seeing a new horizon to start my own company, I asked my boss for permission to pursue Little Jimmy's business. With my boss's blessing, I quit and started my own warehousing business with Little Jimmy as my first customer and Chester as my business partner.

One of Little Jimmy's primary products was supersacks, which arrived at our facility double stacked in shipping containers. The supersacks continued to pile up for about two months. Then it was time for Little Jimmy's product to start leaving our warehouse. There were two possibilities for shipping out the supersacks. The first was to divide the double-stacked bags onto individual pallets, and the second was to ship them out via bulk tankers.

Little Jimmy showed us how to empty the bags into the hopper (a large funnel with a vacuum hose connected to the bottom), where to position the bag, and other specifics. His driver was responsible for opening the bag, but it was up to us to handle the forklifting.

Somehow, one operation went poorly. With Mutt on the forklift and Little Jimmy standing next to the hopper, a pallet came off the forks and hit Little Jimmy on the head, giving him a bloody gash. We patched him up. Mutt and Little Jimmy pointed fingers at each other. But we learned. We refined the process by securing pallets to the forklift mast with rope before lifting it above the hopper. We also decided to keep Little Jimmy away from active operations. The last thing we needed was for our one and only customer to have more accidents.

Even though our relationship with Little Jimmy had its difficulties, he needed us to consolidate his freight into one warehouse, and we needed a customer for our startup, so we both swiped right. However, Chester and I knew from the outset that we needed other customers, and the sooner the better.

Prospecting for New Customers

I put on my best suit and tie. I doublechecked my list of destinations, names, addresses and phone numbers. I kissed my wife and kids and hit the road. I headed out to the "valley" where a string of warehouses and office complexes beckoned with the potential for new freight.

Hands sweating for fear of cold calling, I pulled into my first destination and realized that I was looking at a thirty-door warehousing operation. Several company names adorned the building, but the brokerage company that I hoped to talk with was clearly in bed with another warehousing company. This was not apparent in my online searches. I drove away in disgust and headed to the next place on my list.

Despite some setbacks, I was learning to identify, connect with, and sell new business. Chester and I had experience in the warehouse industry, but we were unfamiliar with the market we had just entered. Our transition had moved us into the international freight market, and the game was different, like the difference between arena football and traditional football. Many fundamentals are the same in both markets, but many of the rules, and the style of play, are distinct. Chester and I knew many people and customers, but they were mostly in the Jones Act market, which we hoped to avoid. The international market was much bigger. But how could we find customers in that arena?

First, I signed up for a trial membership with a bill of lading (BOL) aggregator. These folks, for the low price of $2500 per year, provided memberships that allowed me to look at ports around the world and see copies of the bills of lading submitted by shippers. I do not know how they got copies of this information, but in general the BOLs identified the shipper, consignee, and the payor.

Now I could see the names of international freight companies. Ports in other states or countries would not help me, so I could eliminate them. Also, contrary to my first assumption, I soon discovered that big shipping firms like UPS often needed services from small warehousing companies. But we did not have months to figure out how to navigate the complex UPS world. We needed more business as quickly as we could get it.

I also eliminated specialty companies that would not need warehouse services. Examples included apple exporters, grain exporters, and other commodity exporters who shipped products directly from farmers to the ports. We correctly assumed (there's that word again) that we had nothing to offer those folks.

At the end of the day, I realized that most of the companies listed in the aggregated BOL information would not be a good fit for our services. So, I pulled a few company names out of the list that I could contact during my free trial, gleaned as much information as I could, and then canceled the subscription.

Next, I jumped on the internet and typed in "international freight shippers." That gave me all sorts of information about people to call and visit. I snooped on every website to collect email addresses, phone numbers, and local office locations. Most of these targets were shippers known as "brokers." They work with smaller businesses that don't have in-house employees who can handle international shipping requirements. Lumber mills exporting to Thailand, mom and pop retailers importing from China, and a ton of other small companies do not have the international shipping expertise. The brokers serve that role.

Brokers can be helpful and a pain in the rear. They usually only have a phone and an email address. They often lack experience with operations. Their favorite question is, "Why can't you do this (impossible) thing?" However, they paid us to serve their customers, so we worked with them. With some exceptions, we found some good brokers with whom we could develop a relationship and establish long-term business.

Once we had our list of prospects, Chester and I began making calls, sending emails, and showing up at nearby brokers' offices to establish new business. Most of the responses fit in one of three categories: we do not need warehouse services; we already have a warehouse lined up; we'll let you know if we need anything.

Unfortunately, we never got the following response: "Sure,

I have a ton of freight and need a warehouse for it; here's all my money." It would have been easy to get discouraged, but I knew that business-to-business (B2B) sales is more like being a corn farmer than a dairy farmer. Corn farmers plant seed and then wait for the sun and water to bring up the crop. Zillions of things can go wrong. Sometimes the seed never takes root. Most of the time it never takes root. Crows eat the seeds. The farmer accidentally steps on the shoots, or he underwaters or overwaters the seeds. Whatever the case, the seeds usually do not grow into healthy stalks. Business-to-business sales is like that. It's a lot easier to be a dairy farmer, even a mediocre one. You just keep feeding the cow and pulling on its tits. The milk always flows—as long as you don't try to milk the bull.

Sometimes it felt like we were milking the bull. But we persevered. As a member of local transportation clubs, I hit up people in those circles to see if I might land new business. We called people we knew. We called people who knew other people. "How did you get my number?" was a common refrain. We called up former employers. We asked Mutt what he thought. We talked to the local port authority. We talked to our vendors. We talked to Little Jimmy. We talked to our competitors. Chester talked to his seatmates on airplane trips.

We hunted for customers everywhere we could, in every way that we could think of. It was tough. People in the international market did not know us. They realized we were small, and new to the market. Our limitations became obvious to our prospects. Telling people "We can't do that" felt terrible. All we could do was keep planting seeds.

I also made sure we had a Google profile with updated information. This was important for customers looking for warehousing, and so that truckers could find our address. I had set up a website for Joel's Warehouse and I made sure to regularly blog useful information. I projected a reputable online presence but did not reveal that we were a startup with minimal resources.

Some Seeds Will Sprout

Thankfully, after being in business for two months, we received our first load from a customer not named Little Jimmy. The new business had come to us from a referral, not a direct contact. That began a trend that continued throughout the existence of our warehousing company. Almost all new business came from referrals.

From a psychological perspective, that makes sense. No one likes to listen to cold calls from a stranger. But if they get a referral from someone they know, it lends instant credibility to the third party.

A few seeds we planted did grow, but in their own time. Sometimes a broker would send a customer to us. If someone called us for help with work we could not handle (e.g., rail and refrigerated), we would refer him to a competitor. In return, the competitor would send customers that he could not handle to us.

Some of our previous prospects eventually called us to ask for help. They all had my cellphone number and Chester's.

We may have been small, but we always treated our prospects with an individualized touch (figuratively).

Once new business started coming in, we had to figure out how to handle the work.

Just Do It, or Not

Warehousing is not like running a restaurant. At a restaurant, customers show up and order from the menu. Customers can ask for some variations (no pickles), but generally they will not show up at a Burger King and try to order Thai.

In the warehousing business, customers tell you what they need, and then you tell them whether you can or can't do what they ask. Some potential customers made the error of asking us, "What can you do" or, "Tell me your price for a transload." I always countered with, "Tell me what you need, and I'll tell you if I can do it and for how much. And if I can't do it, then I will refer you to someone who can."

I was obviously afraid of losing future business by referring people elsewhere. But it was an honest and straight-shooting way to interact with potential clients, a risk we sometimes had to take. And sometimes our referrals did not cut us out of future business. People appreciated our honesty and then called us for advice about who could handle other needs. Sometimes the answer was Joel's Warehouse.

We had a reasonable decision-making matrix.

1. If the only business the customer had was refrigerated or rail, or something else that we would never be able to handle, we referred them to appropriate competitors.
2. If the freight was a mix of heavy stuff and warehouse stuff, we would broker the heavy stuff with our buddy down the road and handle the warehouse stuff ourselves.
3. If there were a few containers of refrigerated product that didn't need long-term storage, we would quickly handle the transload from one refrigerated unit to the next.
4. If the job involved a large volume but required specialized forklift equipment, we would bid on it.
5. If the work required specialized equipment, but the volume was small, we would make a judgment call about whether to broker it or refer it. Generally, we hated to broker these loads. They were the worst-case scenario: low profit margin, but a lot of work.

For example, we bid annually for a huge amount of business that involved warehousing rolls of uncut paper. Every year, someone else got the job. This occurred for one simple reason: We were not set up to do this type of work. We did not have the space or the right equipment. As a result, we had to up the price of our bids to pay for an additional warehouse, two specialized forklifts, and two more employees. That made us more expensive than the competitors.

We also could not handle slip-sheet business, products weighing over twelve thousand pounds, anything that required an overhead lift, most hazardous items, bulk cement, etc. We turned away more business than we accepted, which was probably a good thing . . . probably.

So, as you launch your startup, remember a little lesson from your friend Joel. It is better to turn away business that you can't do than to try to do it and fail. It's important to understand your capabilities and limitations.

Saying No

Saying no to money is hard for a business professional, especially one who is launching a startup that is starving for money. But here we were, turning away new business or firing existing customers. Every decision to reject money was painful.

Nevertheless, we wanted to stay focused on our identity as a company and what we could do best. We were always willing to listen to prospective customers, to see if we could find a solution, but the clarity we had about our vision and capacity saved us and our potential clients a lot of time.

Our vision and capacity did evolve and mature over time. As we gained experience, we felt confident that we could take on some new types of work. For example, we picked up a new customer, the Aussie, because he was driving around the port one day and saw that we had a ramp at the warehouse. The Aussie imported vehicles from, well, Australia. His vehicles were designed for rugged, outback use. The steering wheels were on the wrong side, the muffler and exhaust pipe ran above the cab, and they had a vague military surplus design.

The vehicles would come to us in a shipping container

and then we would unload them into the warehouse. Then the Aussie would pick them up with his flatbed trailer. To fit three vehicles in a forty-foot container, someone designed a rack system that would allow one vehicle to be suspended above the others.

Under the principles of "we need money" and "we can probably do that safely" we established a price with the Aussie. A few days later, we sent a truck to the port to pick up the first container.

Operationally, this was an all-hands-on-deck situation. We had to remove blocking and bracing. The forklifts had to tow the lower two vehicles out of the container. The racking system that suspended the third vehicle was on wheels, but everything was somewhat unstable. It all had to be half rolled, half dragged out of the container—with the vehicle suspended. Then we would position a forklift on each side of the elevated vehicle, find appropriate places underneath it for the forks, and carefully do a simultaneous lift. Then we could dismantle the racking system before lowering the vehicle to the ground.

Over the following months, we handled dozens of vehicles this way, but there was no way to turn this into routine and comfortable work. Every vehicle was different. Some had flat tires, some were shells to be rebuilt, some did not have steering wheels. But they all worried us as we dragged and lifted and pushed these vehicles around to get them out of the warehouse.

Most of my "freight-mares" involved unloading vehicles. The worst involved a little yellow 1980s two-seater Porsche in pristine condition. The tires had been flattened to make the vehicle shorter and easier to fit into the shipping container. It had a short wheelbase, which left us with few locations for positioning the forks underneath it. It would have to be a one-forklift operation.

After some discussion, Chester and I decided the only way to get the Porsche off the suspension rack safely required the use of what I referred to as "my girlfriend Britney." Chester always called them "the Spears." Normal warehousemen call them "fork extensions." These pieces of metal extended the standard forks of our five-thousand-pound lift.

"Britney" got a regular workout in our warehouse. For longer pieces of freight, the Spears could provide more stability. When we needed to reach the handles of supersacks that were slightly out of the reach of the normal forks, we would use the Spears. However, they had two major drawbacks: They were not solid steel and therefore could bear only a limited amount of weight, and, by adding length to the forks, they created potential leverage issues.

Successful forklift operators must understand leverage and center of gravity by gut instinct. These physical factors are not something that can be gauged scientifically. Forklift drivers do not typically have master's degrees in mathematics, nor do they have hours to figure out complex equations. When you start handling a piece of unknown freight, you *feel through the forklift* where the center of gravity is, and what is going to happen when you start picking up the object.

More specifically, when an operator is driving a five-thousand-pound forklift, he realizes that he must position the freight at a low center of gravity; that is, low and close to the forklift mast. If the operator tries to lift something that weighs five thousand pounds by using only the tips of the forks, the back of the forklift might come off the ground. So, by using Britney to lift a wider or longer piece of freight, the operator has to understand that the center of gravity will be farther away from the forklift. If you would like to visualize my description, you can search YouTube for forklift fails. You'll see leverage fails along with other freight disasters.

To handle the Porsche, we used Britney. Chester volunteered to operate the forklift. Mutt and I helped guide him under the car, with the forks positioned close together to accommodate the short wheelbase.

As he initiated the lift, the vehicle rocked gently. It was balanced precariously on a fulcrum. We all held our breath.

Mutt, Juan Carlos, and I worked as fast as we could to dismantle the racking. We broke apart the pieces and pulled the racking away. Then Chester eased the Porsche gently toward the ground. This was the most dangerous part of the procedure because the hydraulics on a forklift don't always provide a smooth lift or descent. Chester successfully lowered the Porsche, after what felt like an eternity. Disaster averted.

I had nightmares about that operation for months. It impacted Chester, too. We agreed that we should stop handling vehicles. So, when the Aussie came to pick up another shipment of his vehicles, we told him to find a different warehouse. We were gentle but firm. The Aussie was disappointed, but he understood.

Our Second Regular Customer

Broker A2Z, whose main offices were located only a few minutes from our warehouse, became our second regular customer. Over the years, they brought us all sorts of interesting business and referrals. They had offices all over the US, so we also developed relationships with several of their locations.

We got a shot with them because we could say yes to work that their other warehouse didn't want to do. A2Z worked with an engineering firm that shipped hard-to-find machinery parts around the world. If someone needed a rotor for a 1970s-era Soviet military helicopter, they could find it, inspect it, and ship it wherever it needed to go.

However, the engineering firm had a problem. A customer in the Middle East had ordered an expensive cockpit flight simulator, and for some reason that customer decided to ship it back to them. The simulator came in three large crates and one large skid. A2Z asked us to store the simulator for the engineering firm while they figured out what to do with it.

It's better to not know certain things. I did not want to know the value of the simulator. We placed it in a corner of the warehouse far from the flow of freight and forklift traffic. For the next two and a half years, the simulator didn't move. It became just another warehouse fixture, like it was part of the wall. Occasionally, we would remind each other that the simulator was still there, gathering dust. We joked that we needed to put it together and charge admission for people to use it. But we got paid monthly like clockwork.

A2Z introduced us to a wide array of clients and products, such as a dollar store company based in the Midwest and a video game tournament business that hosted conventions all over the world. They also had us regularly prepare a jam concentrate for air shipping to Asia, unload containers of expensive machine-shop equipment, and unload containers full of hand-stacked knickknacks for some company called Amazon.

The amazing thing about being in warehousing is that we had no idea what we would get into next.

4

Your Products and Services Define You

I debated whether to include this chapter in the book because it gets into the weeds of freight transportation. I realize that most of you reading the book are not in the same industry. However, I think the chapter is important, for two reasons. First, the freight we handled often dictated our business decisions, and I suspect that your product or service will determine many of your decisions. Second, the freight industry affects us all deeply, as the global supply chain problems in 2021 and 2022 attest. Everyone will benefit from a deeper understanding of this industry.

So, please bear with me as I go down the rabbit hole.

The Freight Made the Business

Our success as a warehousing company hinged on our ability to handle freight effectively and safely. Sometimes we could also measure success by the freight we declined to move. Likewise, your startup will have requirements tied to the product or service you are selling. That will impact all your decisions—about your company location, the materials you buy, who you hire, and how you conduct business.

Our choice of warehouses was dictated by Little Jimmy's freight. Had he needed rail services, we would have looked for a warehouse with rail access. Subsequent expansion of warehouse space was also dictated by the freight we handled. At times we considered getting a specific type of warehouse (e.g., refrigerated) and then trying to find the freight to fill it. But that was too risky. The freight came first, then we chose the warehouse.

Our initial two forklifts included one five-thousand-pound "Speedboat" model with 42-inch forks and a six-thousand-pound "Tank," also with 42-inch forks. The Tank was better at unloading containers with double-stacked pallets of supersacks. The Speedboat, with its narrow forks, was better at grabbing the handles of bags used for bulk loadouts. Both forklifts could perform both duties, but there were advantages to using each for specific tasks. As we grew, the new forklifts would become even more specialized in relation to the freight.

The 42-inch length of the forks is not standard. Most forklifts automatically come with 48-inch forks to accommodate the standard pallet dimensions of 40 by 48 inches. Supersack pallets are smaller, so standard 48-inch forks make it more likely to damage the supersacks behind the pallet a driver is trying to grab. As with sex, horseshoes, and hand grenades, the freight world is often a game of inches.

Subsequent decisions related to forklifts, tools, and future warehouse expansion were determined by the freight, not the other way around. The freight also directly impacted our hiring decisions.

The nature of the freight business forced us to be adaptable. Due to the complexity of global commerce, the industry is an extremely complicated machine that has no central architect. Somehow all the cogs in the machine work together to make our lives possible, even though the industry is constantly evolving and adapting. Cogs appear and disappear, get larger and smaller, and move around the machine to hook up to different cogs all the time. Yet somehow it consistently produces positive results.

The Freight World Is Complex

Without freight transportation, most of us would die. That is not an exaggeration. The industry enables us to survive in the modern world. Food at the grocery store, fuel at the gas station, medications, and hospital supplies—nearly every product requires a complex global system.

I am by no means an expert in every facet of freight transportation. I know how to drive a forklift and yard hostler, but not a tractor-trailer. No one wants me behind the wheel of an eighteen-wheeler moving down the freeway at sixty miles per hour. In fact, I do not think there are any experts in freight transportation. Every cog in the machine has its experts, but I do not know of any one person who can understand every cog. But to help you comprehend the complexity of the freight machine, let me explain our role as one cog in the water bottling business. Let's start with how the business originated.

Somewhere in Indonesia, very smart chemists mixed some compounds to generate polyethylene terephthalate (PET) resin. First, some people extracted the raw materials from the ground. Numerous truckers shipped those materials to the PET resin manufacturer in Indonesia. The manufacturer then combined them to create the PET resin and then loaded it into containers. Truckers pulled the containers to the port. The terminal workers loaded the containers onto ships. The shipping line brought it across the ocean. Workers at the destination terminal unloaded the containers off the ships. Then other truckers moved the product out of the port and delivered it to many destinations.

By my guesstimate, at least ten different companies handled this freight before it reached the final users. Depending on the number of raw materials and refineries involved, there might have been thirty companies involved. That doesn't include the suppliers and manufacturers who were responsible for building the trucks, ships, machines, and tools required to create and deliver the PET. All those companies had their own transportation supply lines. It is unbelievably complex.

Our warehouse was one of many companies that handled this product. It sat in our warehouse for a few weeks. Another company picked it up and delivered it to the bottled water plant where workers turned the PET resin into bottles for water. Then more trucks hauled the bottles of water to another offsite warehouse. That warehouse stored the bottles of water until yet another trucker delivered them to a store for final sale. There, a consumer purchased a two-dozen pack of bottled water for $3.99. That $3.99 purchase supported dozens of companies and tens of thousands of employees around the world. It's amazing.

Imagine how many transportation companies are involved in supporting the hundreds of thousands of products in millions of locations all over the US. The system is mind boggling, and terrifyingly fragile. Imagine how much our lives would change if needed products could not make it to grocery store shelves, or if you could not buy simple appliances like toasters from Walmart.

According to the book titled *The Toaster Project*, a guy named Thomas Thwaites tried to reverse engineer a toaster he bought for 3.99 British pounds (just over $5). Nine months and more than $1300 later, he plugged in his finished product and watched it melt. Another article published on the Gizmodo site stated that the "simple" toaster was made of four hundred parts, built with over one hundred raw materials. Thwaites could not source many of those materials locally in the UK. It's no wonder that his effort failed.

Thankfully, we just needed to fulfill our small role of handling the freight in front of us.

How Do You Want It?

Sometimes the supersacks left our warehouse on pallets. Then they were loaded into outbound trailers in a stable formation of one 2500-pound sack for each pallet. To separate double-stacked sacks and place one on each pallet, the forklift driver had to snake the forks through the handles on the top bag, lift it off, and then lower it onto a fresh pallet. It was not always that easy. The handles often lay flat against the top, making it difficult to get the forks under the handles. The tops of the double-stacked bags were over seven feet off the ground, so sometimes the driver or an assistant "bag man" had to jump off the forklift and go up a ladder. Mutt often wandered into the office looking for someone to "grab 'em by the ears" while he rode the bull.

That was usually my cue to drop what I was doing on the computer and assist him. While I was standing on a ladder grabbing handles, Mutt would talk to me constantly about sports, weather, politics, golf swings, and whatever else would pop into his head.

"You know why you grab 'em by the ears right?" He would holler at me when the rest of the conversation got stale.

"Why?" I'd ask, as though I hadn't heard this explanation a thousand times before.

"To keep 'em where you want 'em." Then he would mimic getting a blowjob. I'd express my disgust while he drove off laughing.

Loading supersacks onto over-the-road trailers was not the simplest task either. Each pallet weighed almost 2500 pounds.

The trailers had weight limitations of between 44,000 to 45,000 pounds. In addition to worrying about weight limits, we had to make sure that the weight was legally distributed in the trailer. The law requires freight haulers to keep weight off the truck and trailer axles so as to prevent excessive wear on road surfaces or damage to bridges.

Weight distribution was often problematic. We usually loaded eighteen bags per outbound trailer for an estimated total weight of 43,000 to 45,000 pounds. No two bags were the same, so we had to watch for weight variations. A variation of 2 percent of approximately 2500 pounds could lead to nine hundred pounds of excess weight when measured at a truck scale.

It was a juggling act. We wanted to load to the upper weight limit while trying to arrange the freight so as to keep weight off the axles. Thirty standard-size pallets could fit in a fifty-three-foot trailer, but the pallets for supersacks were not standard. They were slightly smaller, which gave us approximately thirty pallet spots. However, we could only legally load eighteen pallets without exceeding weight limitations. Moreover, each truck and trailer has its own unique weight. Fuel quantities, or even the driver's personal effects, can add hundreds of pounds to the truck's weight. All these factors must be considered when putting freight into a trailer, and I have not even discussed what is required for fragile or hazardous materials.

To resolve our loading challenges, we always sought direction from the truck driver. We reasoned that the drivers would know the truck and trailer better than anyone, and they were the ones who got the tickets if they broke weight rules. Most drivers had some idea about how to distribute pallets within trailers.

Often our configurations would leave a little less than eight feet of space at the back of the trailer. The driver would throw a load bar across the last set of pallets to prevent the bags from sliding farther toward the back of the trailer. There are other systems that serve this function, such as those that have metal slots running vertically inside the trailer walls. Load bars fasten to these metal slots. The built-in track systems are more secure, but they make it harder to adapt to each load. Positioning a bar two feet from the freight means the freight could gain momentum before busting through the bar.

In general, loading supersacks into trailers was easier than a second method—bulk loading. Bulk loading was time consuming, loud, and had high potential for disaster.

Bulk Loading

Bulk loads—loading without supersacks, and only with loose product—required a lot of non-standard equipment. First, the tractor has to be modified to provide power for a vacuum and blower system. The tractor is vented via a muffler that barely dampens the noise of the PTO (power take off), which is the energy source for the vacuum and blower. The PTO needs to idle during the entirety of the loadout, but the sound of the blower makes it impossible to hear it.

The trailer is hooked up to the truck with a series of stainless-steel hoses at least eight inches in diameter. The vacuum and blower system then builds up pressure inside the trailer tank to create the suction needed to either fill the tank or expel product from the trailer at the customer's location. When fully loaded, bulk tankers might carry more than fifty-five thousand pounds of product.

At our warehouse, the bulk tanker would be connected by a stainless-steel hose to a hopper located inside the building. The hoppers were approximately seven feet tall, large enough to hold two supersacks of product. Once a vacuum had built up inside the bulk tanker, any product in the hopper would be sucked through the hose and into the truck. There was a multistage filter system to eliminate debris from the product.

The bulk loadout was a two-man job. We provided the forklift driver and the trucking company provided the driver. The driver assisted the forklift driver in grabbing the bag handles. The driver also climbed the stairs next to the hopper and untied the bottom of each supersack so that the product could drain into the hopper. It took roughly an hour and fifteen minutes each time to load between twenty-two and twenty-four bags.

Once the product arrived at the customer's location, the hoses were reconnected and the air flow was reversed, sending the product through the hose and into large silos where it was stored until the manufacturing plant was ready to clean and process it.

There were several ways for a bulk load to go wrong. Most involved the equipment breaking down or, heaven forbid, a hose coming loose and spraying product all over the place. The vacuum and blower system did break down a few times. However, the main concern was operator error leading to injury.

Oops

The frequency with which we connected and disconnected hoses increased the potential for a step to be missed. For example, a driver once pulled the tractor trailer away from the door and, as I watched dumbfounded, yanked the steel hopper out of the warehouse and into the yard. The hopper crashed to the ground with a loud metallic "clang!" Several of us yelled and got the driver to stop, otherwise he would have dragged the hopper through the yard.

The accident caused minor damage to the hopper, but we were lucky that no one was hurt. A forklift operator could have been standing around the hopper or even between the hopper and the warehouse door. Due to the gravity of the situation, we launched an investigation. Did everyone follow our procedures?

It was the driver's responsibility to disconnect the hose that connected the hopper to the bulk trailer. He was an experienced operator who had done hundreds of loads in the past. He simply missed a step, which reminded us that no matter how well we had established safety procedures, honest mistakes can still happen.

In the world of quality management principles, (Six Sigma

for example), the Japanese term *poka-yoke* describes the idea of trying to mistake-proof a process. The best way is to eliminate any chances of human error. For example, diesel pumps at gas stations are designed so that the nozzle is too large to fit into the receptacle of a gasoline-powered car. This makes it practically impossible for someone to make that mistake, but it doesn't stop someone with a diesel-powered car from filling a tank with gasoline. Gas pumps also have breakaway hoses. If someone forgets to remove the nozzle from the car and tries to drive off, the hose will disconnect. In these ways, gas stations have made it difficult for human mistakes to cause serious damage, but they cannot plan for everything. A vehicle traveling at high speed could still hit the pumps from the side and dislodge them. Vehicles have also plowed into the attached convenience stores.

Gas station owners put their money into preventing common accidents. A *New York Times* article in 2010 stated that drivers pull away with nozzles attached once per month per gas station. With over one hundred thousand gas stations in the US, that seems like an exceptionally large number. If we divide by thirty days in a month, that would be over three thousand times per day. Whatever the case, I think it is fair to say that it is a common occurrence.

This leads back to our accident with the hopper. What was the underlying cause of the mistake and was there a way to prevent it from happening again?

After the accident, we looked for clues. The driver insisted that he had disconnected the hose from the truck. It was hard not to believe him, but we had a hopper that had just flown out of the warehouse, and it had been attached to the trailer somehow. The driver, Chester, and I stood around and discussed it for a while and finally pieced together what we think happened.

The stainless-steel hoses we used in these operations are not very flexible. They will bend a little, but at eight inches in diameter they can't be folded. Wrestling with one can feel a bit like fighting a ten-foot anaconda. We concluded that the driver had indeed disconnected the hose from the truck as he claimed, but that he had failed to shove the hose completely back into the warehouse. The hose had flopped over and one of the clamp pieces snagged on a support rod at the back of the trailer.

After that accident, the drivers and forklift operators made sure that the hose was completely back in the warehouse before the truck pulled away from the dock. The cameras caught part of the incident (not the cause), so I was able to repeatedly watch the hopper flying out of the warehouse.

Exceptional vs. Transactional

My experience in warehousing has shown me that there are very few "transactional" relationships. I can't think of a single business interaction during which I did not sense a human connection. That is the difference between being in a business-to-business relationship versus being in a business-to-consumer relationship. Joel's Warehouse, in that sense, had a more personal relationship with our customers than a

Target store has with theirs.

Business books will often refer to "managing by exception." In theory, these books suggest that most interactions should be routine (transactional), and that the remaining time and energy should be spent on exception management. I suspect that the actual percentages vary widely by industry.

The concept is generally valid, but in our case we had very little "routine" work. We had more than fifty customers. We strove to figure out how we should serve each customer's particular needs, and then we tried to consistently meet those expectations.

For example, we could never feel routinely comfortable with the Aussie. Every time we opened one of his containers, we had to treat his vehicles as if they were our only freight. The stakes were too high, and the configuration of the vehicles was different each time. Even when we weren't actively unloading his containers, the freight-mares were taking up valuable brain space for Chester and me.

Conversely, we had a customer who routinely (once or twice per month) ordered canned and jarred goods from a Fortune 500 food processor. Our job was to receive the freight, inspect it for damage, change the labels on it to hide the source, relabel it for our customer, and a couple of days later reload it for the destination customer (usually a small grocery chain). To discover damage, we had to investigate pallets of product to see if there were any signs of condensation within the shrink wrap. If so, we had to tear the pallet apart and find the broken jars or cans and then rebuild the pallets without the spoiled product. We then reported any damages to our customer so he could file a claim with the food processor.

While this customer's loads came with a specific routine, the routine didn't apply to any of our other customers. There were some common elements, such as making sure the drivers had the correct outbound bill of lading, but this customer's unique freight required its own processes. Each of our fifty-plus customers had a unique need that required us to individualize our freight-handling processes.

I think (hope) that our customers loved us for the way we always handled their needs in a specialized manner.

5

Communication

In all business, communication is key. In fact, good communication can save your bacon. This is true regardless of whom you are dealing with, including customers, vendors, accountants, employees, the FBI, or a homeless guy. In business, we should communicate to clarify expectations, convey progress, and to provide the post-game summary.

Clarifying Expectations

When dealing with customers, they need to clearly express their needs and we need to accurately convey what we can do. The process needs to be repeated until everyone understands the expectations. If they are not clear, then a world of problems can emerge.

For example, we needed customers to tell us the exact specifications of their shipments. We needed to know sizes and weights, shipment arrival times, duration of storage, type of product, and inbound and outbound trucking needs. If we were lucky, all the information sent to us would match up with Reality. However, Reality often involved a screw up. The ship might arrive three days early and so the port would start charging for container storage unless we immediately picked it up. The trucker designated for that work might still be enroute from Middle of Nowhere, North Dakota. In short, one problem would set off a domino effect causing a litany of other problems.

Chester often said that "an emergency on your part doesn't create a sense of urgency on mine." But in Reality, we liked money and so we would jump through many hoops to keep our clients happy despite the situation. We tried to communicate well with clients, reminding them that warehousing involves many unpredictable moving pieces. That way, if a problem in Reality occurred, we could minimize the chances of them being upset with us.

When problems emerged and the domino effect set in, damage control seemed more complicated than a moon landing. Here's a common scenario. Chester and I made a few calls to find a truck in line at the port. Trucker 1 was willing to pick up our container first, but he thought he had a two-hour wait before he could get out of the port. Our warehouse was located about five minutes outside the terminal gates, so we thought the driver would arrive in about two hours.

Thirty minutes later, the broker called us for an update and learned about the two-hour port delay. The broker called his customer and spread blame for the delay. Meanwhile, trucker 2 showed up to haul out the freight coming from trucker 1. We told trucker 2 that trucker 1 was stuck at the port and would probably arrive in an hour, adding that he could wait in his truck at door four until the freight arrived. Trucker 2 called his dispatcher to say the freight wasn't ready. The dispatcher called the consignee and told him that the warehouse was too busy to load the freight from trucker 1. The consignee called the broker and bitched him out.

Next, I got a call from the broker. He was upset because he mistakenly thought that we put trucker 2 in the back of the queue. I calmly explained that trucker 1 was still in the port and that we expected to see the container in about an hour. I further explained that trucker 2 knew this fact, and that we had him sitting at door four so that the load could be transferred immediately upon arrival. The broker was mollified and said that "the dispatcher is stupid" and then hung up. He then called the consignee and told them some version of the truth.

See what I mean about communication?

Convey Progress

This case study is not over. After an hour of peace between phone calls, the container from trucker 1 showed up. Turns out the broker had the wrong information about the container's contents. Instead of eighteen crates in the container, there was one long crate that weighed eighteen thousand pounds, according to the packing slip. It was a large screw for an electricity generating windmill in a single crate, not a bunch of small screws in small crates.

I called the broker and explained the issue. We haggled,

but it slowly dawned on him that he had been reading the paperwork wrong and making wrong assumptions about inches instead of feet. "I thought it was a typo," the broker said. "I didn't think it would actually be thirty-six feet long." Then he wanted to know what *we* were going to do about it, adding that it had to be shipped out immediately.

I did not make any promises. I warned him that the charges would have to change, and that we might even send the container to a different facility. He told me to do whatever was necessary to get the job done and that he would cover the charges.

We were in a tough spot. Even though it was not our fault, we wanted to do whatever we could to help the broker. We had a couple of options. I called a friend who specialized in lifting full containers and other heavy freight. His biggest forklift could handle one hundred thousand pounds, so I hoped that he could find a way to drag the container out of the inbound trailer and place it in the outbound trailer.

Meanwhile, Chester was on the twelve-thousand-pound forklift, which we affectionately nicknamed "the Beast." He was using the sixty-inch lumber forks to lift the back end of the crate, but the Beast was no match for a crate weighing eighteen thousand pounds. Chester then came up with the idea of securing chains to the crate's underside runners and to the forklift's mast.

We cleared out of his way. Chester started to back out of the container, lifting the crate a bit more to reduce the drag. The crate started to move, sliding relatively easily on the container's wood floor. As he backed down the steel deck plates, we saw a new problem: There wasn't thirty-six feet of warehouse space behind him to completely remove the crate. Mutt jumped on the five-thousand-pound forklift, which he called "the Speedboat," while our newest hire, Juan Carlos, jumped on the six-thousand-pound forklift known as the Tank.

Mutt and Juan Carlos started to clear space behind Chester by moving supersacks, pallets of mattresses, small crates of machinery, and other items out of the way. Then Chester restarted the effort to remove the crate; however, now the runners were stuck on something. He revved the Beast's engine and shoved the crate about six inches back into the container. Then he reversed direction, slowly backing out with momentum. The crate slid out, down the steel dock plate, and onto the floor of the warehouse.

Keeping my mind on the importance of communication, I stayed busy taking pictures of the operation, mainly to have proof of our efforts in case someone tried to file a damage claim. I also wanted to prove to the broker that we had one massive crate, not eighteen small crates. With the crate successfully removed from the container, I called the broker with a progress report.

We had staged the inbound container at door three and the outbound trailer at door four. Mutt and Juan Carlos used their forklifts to help Chester slide the long crate across a dozen feet. We gently lined the crate up with the outbound trailer and Chester pushed it in. The outbound trailer was fifty-three feet long, so Chester pushed the crate all the way to the front. We disconnected the chains and Chester backed the Beast of out of the trailer. The driver threw a load bar in front of the crate to keep it from sliding during transit. We were done with everything but the paperwork.

Provide a Post-Game Summary

I called the broker to tell him we had successfully completed the job, adding that he owed us more money for misdescribing the freight and forcing us to throw a bunch of resources at it. He agreed to throw in another $200 and expressed his gratitude for how quickly we got it done. When he saw the photos of the crate, he sent an inane reply: "That's big." I was tempted to send a comment like, "No shit," but instead I typed out something equally inane like, "Have a great day! Thanks for using us! Call me anytime!"

Back to work. We had been ignoring the other drivers for the previous forty-five minutes. We had containers parked at every door and a traffic jam in the parking lot. I started shuffling bills of lading, making calls, and directing traffic while Chester and the others started unloading or loading the containers.

Who? What? Where? When?

The song "More Than a Feeling" by Boston started playing on my phone as I woke up in the middle of the night. Blurrily I checked the time. It was 2:15 a.m. "Hello?" I answered groggily.

"Uh, yeah, hi. My name's Tom. I'm a trucker and I'm scheduled to pick up at your warehouse at 8 a.m. Looks like I'm going to arrive a bit early, and I was wondering if I could park in your lot and catch a few hours of sleep."

It took a bit for my mind to start working, but I soon remembered that our lot was secured behind a fence. With a mumble, I suggested that he could go around the corner and park on the shoulder. I added that we would open the gate at about 7:30 a.m. He apologized for calling at such an hour. I assured him that it was not a problem.

I have always been nice to long-haul truckers. Many people consider trucking to be a stupid, easy job. However, most people would not trade places with them, even though long-haul drivers make a good living. Do you know what you call a profession that pays well but has a constant shortage of workers? Hard.

Communication can be a real pain in the rear for truckers. When a widget maker in China loads a container and sends it to the port, they include information about the container's contents, about the shipper, and about the payor and consignee. Many times, the shipper only has the address for a freight broker in some downtown high-rise building. The widget maker simply uses the broker's address to get the freight out the door.

The broker will then call a warehouseman like myself and provide information to pick up the container at the port. I dispatch a truck to the terminal. When the container arrives, I let the broker know and ask him when the outbound trucker will pick it up from the warehouse. Depending on the answer, I determine where to put the freight in the warehouse. If the broker says he wants to move the shipment quickly, he immediately starts looking for an outbound trucker.

Soon I get a call from a trucker.

"Hey, I guess I'm supposed to pick up from you," the driver says, "but I was told this number was for Benny's Brokerage."

"I'm familiar with Benny's Brokerage. This is Joel's Warehouse. Do you know what commodity you're picking up?"

The truck driver, trying to keep his eyes on the road while reading texts messages from his dispatcher, says, "They didn't tell me."

"Any idea where it is going?"

"They tell me I'm going to Texas, but I'm not sure exactly where in Texas."

I rack my brain, trying to connect the broker with freight bound for somewhere in Texas. "I'm not sure what the freight is, but I'll call Benny's Brokerage and find out. Do you know how to get to the warehouse?"

"No clue," the driver admits. "They said to call you and ask."

I ask the driver where he is and realize he's probably two hours south of us on the freeway. I give him the directions and remind him to look for the sign for Joel's Warehouse and to turn into the second gate, which is the entrance. I emphasize that he should not use the first gate because that is only for outbound traffic.

Next, I call the broker and figure out which freight the

trucker should pick up and the exact destination address. If the driver is lucky, the rest of his trip will be trouble free. He'll pick up the freight, head to Texas, deliver the load, and then be on to the next one. However, there are many ways that his life can go wrong.

For starters, there are the bridge laws. These are the legal weight limits that tractor-trailer combos can carry. As described earlier, the weight limits are not easily determined. So, we tried to arrange freight inside their trailer to keep the weight off the axles and toward the center of the trailer.

To avoid tickets, over-the-road truckers try to keep the cargo weight between forty-two thousand and forty-five thousand pounds on a standard two-axle, fifty-three-foot trailer. However, the rules in port areas usually allow a twenty-foot container to hold fifty-thousand pounds or more of product. They usually reach the warehouses uncontested. As you can imagine, that often creates mismatches between the amount of weight we can receive at the warehouse versus the amount of weight the truck driver can haul away.

Sometimes the weights listed by the shipper or broker are not accurate. If that happens, drivers often need to return to the warehouse to remove pallets or crates. We met drivers who had to come back three times to have us reposition freight. Although we worked with the drivers to properly position the loads, it was anyone's guess whether a plan would work. Smart drivers would spend a few bucks at a nearby weigh scale to make sure they were legal before heading out on a two-thousand-mile drive.

In other words, truckers often face added hardship due to

poor communication. With so many people in the mix—the shipper, port trucker, warehouse, broker, consignee, long-haul trucker, and long-haul dispatcher—there is plenty of room for mistakes and finger pointing.

Finger Pointing

No one likes to make mistakes, but we dislike assuming responsibility for mistakes even more. In the freight industry, most mistakes are errors of omission, which is why I stress the importance of communication. The more information everyone has, the easier it is to avoid mistakes and salvage them if they occur.

Poor communication caused the worst dispatching mistake I ever saw. It happened when our company had grown from twenty-five thousand square feet to sixty-five thousand square feet, spread across two buildings. Instead of one customer, we had more than fifty.

Little Jimmy was still our number one customer. At the time, we were shipping out a hundred loads of his supersacks onto over-the-road trucks heading toward a small city in California. This project had been going on for days, and we had been loading eight to ten trucks per day.

When a driver showed up, I asked him what he was picking up and where he was going. He did not have the slightest clue. All he had was a number written down on a piece of paper. I could not match it to anything, so I asked him to contact his dispatcher and give me more information.

This scenario was not unusual. It took forty minutes, but the driver came back and said he was going to Vernon, California.

I gave him a bill of lading for Little Jimmy's supersacks to Vernon and directed him to go to our second warehouse (same block but around the corner). I informed the forklift driver there that a truck was on the way. Mutt was at that warehouse loading outbound trailers. I moved on to other tasks and forgot about the driver.

The next day I got a call from an irate lumber customer asking me what I had done with his lumber. I told him we hadn't shipped out any lumber the day before. The irate customer said he would call me back and hung up.

Next, a dispatcher with a truck brokerage called to say that I had loaded a truck heading to Vernon, California with the wrong product. Confused, I told him that I was in the middle of a hundred-load project with trucks going to Vernon, California.

You can see where this is going. I had a lumber customer who decided to move some product to Vernon, California the same week that I was moving a hundred loads of supersacks to the same city. It was a horrible coincidence.

At the heart of the problem was poor communication. The driver tried to give me a release number that the lumber customer had sent by email a couple of weeks earlier. The email did not include information about the destination. It also did not tell me anything about the driver's estimated time of arrival, or any other important information.

There were some heated phone calls and discussions that day. Little Jimmy stepped up with an elegant solution. He would pay the driver for taking his supersack load to Vernon. That would free up my lumber customer to hire a driver to move his lumber.

To this day, I am conflicted about who should have been blamed. There was plenty of blame to go around. Had someone, especially *me*, asked one more question, the mistake could have been avoided. As for Chester, his view was, "No way was that your fault. Fuck those guys." Good old Chester. He had my back.

To console myself, I remembered that after thousands of dispatches, we only made one error. But I still dwell on that failure. Perhaps it is human nature to remember the mistakes more than the successes. Whatever the case, this story demonstrates that better communication can prevent mistakes. Communication is a critical factor of running any startup.

6

Employees and Company Culture

Motivating employees is hard. Typically, they are motivated by money, which employers often like to hold on to. So, employers try cheaper tactics, such as giving out company knickknacks, creating "fun committees" with yearly budgets of $250, and trying to convince employees that they are a "family." Maybe these tactics work on some people, but they did not work on me.

As the owner of a startup, you decide how to motivate your employees.

You Can't Do Everything

As I mentioned earlier, you should hire people with different skills than yours. Then be sure to listen to them. To listen does not mean doing everything they say, but it does mean that you take the time to understand their ideas. As the business owner, why hire people who will not challenge you or offer a different perspective? Otherwise, you are assuming that you have all the answers. I can promise that you don't.

No one does.

I am not suggesting you hire people who are the opposite of you, or whose personalities clash just because some jackass named Joel wrote a book saying that you should get different perspectives into your company. Hiring people with complementary skills can and should lead to some friction, but the goal is to make you stronger in areas where you are weak.

As the owner of a startup, you will get used to being a Jack (or Jill) of all trades. At Joel's Warehouse, I cleaned toilets, unloaded containers, threw boxes of mattresses, and signed every employee paycheck. Paying employees, and myself, was my favorite part of the job. But I knew that I could not do everything alone. I certainly could not be an expert in everything. I needed Chester's input about many jobs because he often had ideas that I didn't.

Chester

Chester, besides being my business partner at Joel's Warehouse, had been a customer, a friend, an employee, and a mentor. We did not always see eye to eye, but we faced challenges together.

Born in Canada, Chester thought that his extremely outgoing personality came from his foreign upbringing. Originally, he was a teacher with a master's degree in health. By the time I met him, he was a retired freight guy with thirty years of experience who was now consulting. Chester's friendly approach sometimes got him into trouble.

While having drinks with me at a bar, Chester started a conversation with a couple of gals sitting near us. Pretty soon he was exchanging numbers with one woman who was twenty years younger. She was a travel agent who thought she was lining up a frequent customer. I suspected at the time, because he had done it before, that Chester had given her my phone number as a prank. However, Chester gave her his cell number instead of mine. He soon discovered that she was persistent. She called him at all hours about running his domestic air travel through her business. Eventually, I answered the phone for Chester and told her that he had died of old age. The calls finally stopped, but not before she gave me one last sales pitch. I lied and told her that "I never travel."

Jokes and ribbing were normal parts of our friendship. A few years before we started Joel's Warehouse, Chester showed off his newest purchase in Canada.

"I was visiting relatives over the weekend in Canada and picked up a Tim Horton's coffee mug," he said proudly.

"What's Tim Horton's?" I asked.

"It's like a Dunkin' Donuts, but better," he boasted.

"Nothing good has ever come out of Canada," I told him. "Try to name three things."

"Me, hockey, and . . ."

"Celine Dion," I offered.

"She's *French*-Canadian," he shot back. "That doesn't count."

"Justin Bieber," I said with a smirk.

"I'm a *belieber*," Chester stated. As a man in his late sixties,

Chester was the last person I thought would be a *belieber*. But this revelation gave me an idea.

A couple of days later, he went into his office and discovered it had been decorated like a teenage girl's bedroom: Justin Bieber posters and a Bieber calendar hung on the wall surrounded by pink ribbon and glitter. He took the teasing like a champ. He even left the Bieber swag up for months.

By our third year at Joel's Warehouse, just as we were kicking into high gear, Chester got some concerning news about his health, which meant that he would occasionally miss work. If I encountered a problem container when he was gone, I took a picture and texted it to him. Sometimes he would share an idea for how to handle the job. Sometimes he would suggest that I send the work elsewhere. He made phone calls that I did not have time to make, because I was in the warehouse trying to be him, and in the office trying to be myself. He was involved as much as he could be.

I did not have time to do it all. I did not have all the answers. But I had Chester.

Katie

I had my wife, Katie, in the office a couple of days a week. I needed someone to handle the inventory spreadsheet, bills of lading, and other important paperwork. She was competent at that job and fully motivated. To quote one of my favorite books, she had "skin in the game."

Of course, she made the boss take her out to lunch during

her days at the warehouse. As lunchtime approached, she would text me from her nearby desk. "Feed me, Seymore." I tried to keep a straight face after hearing my cell phone ping, but I knew that it would be perilous to ignore the text. I usually complied.

If you've read any of my other *Surviving* books, you'll know that Katie is my partner in all things. We worked together to start our business, and later to sell our business, and then to sell our house and to move across the country while raising our two boys.

Juan Carlos

Juan Carlos learned quickly. He had that essential gut instinct on the forklift. I showed him one time how to unload containers of supersacks. I gave him pointers about when to tilt the forks to get through the door, how to quickly grab stacks of bags in the right order, and how to avoid damaging freight. One time was enough. We could count on him to reliably handle the loads from that moment on. As with any employee, Juan Carlos was not perfect. But he was such a good forklift driver that we overlooked his minor flaws.

Mutt

Mutt showed up at the warehouse even on his days off—so that he could grab a cup of coffee with us before heading to the golf course. He started at the warehouse two days after we opened. He didn't need the job, but he was willing to work for the laughs, most of which he brought to the workplace. Like Chester, Mutt suffered from an excess of personality, but unlike Chester he wasn't a bulldog that could rip your arm off. He kept up a steady stream of conversation with every driver as he loaded or unloaded the trailers. He would read the newspaper every morning and then share what he read with everyone all day long.

Mutt also had no fear when he was on the forklift. He was a maestro on the machine, getting it to do things that other people would find impossible. This was due to his natural athleticism. When he turned seventy, he started bragging about how he could now shoot his age playing golf. That claim was not just bluster.

MP

I hired MP after we acquired the lumber export business. MP stayed on after the acquisition and continued to manage the lumber export business just like he had for the previous thirty years.

He was the sort of guy who took failure personally. When something went wrong, which was rare, he would turn red. Chester would say, "If MP had any hair left it would have caught on fire."

Like everyone, MP received his share of spam and scammer calls. However, he took delight in talking with those folks while making them think they had a sucker on the line. I once walked into the office and heard him say this to a scammer: "I just pulled into Target and I'm getting the gift card now." MP was supposed to read the gift card numbers to the scammer, who claimed to work for Microsoft, in exchange for removing viruses off his computer.

Soon the scammer called back asking for the card numbers. "I'm standing in line," MP told him. "I'll call you back." Then he hung up.

After a few minutes, the scammer called again and complained about how long it was taking. "That's because I'm not at Target," MP replied.

I could hear the scammer yell, "What!?"

"You're trying to scam me, loser. I'm giving this information to the police."

"Thanks for wasting my time!" the scammer said before hanging up.

"I wasted *his* time?" MP wondered, while shaking his head. "What a jerk."

Terry

Terry was part of the lumber exporting crew with MP. He also stayed on after the acquisition. He was the only guy who wanted to drive the big outdoor forklift, which in my view meant that he had the worst job of all. It was his role to offload flatbeds of incoming lumber, regardless of the weather. He then had to take the lumber to the dirt lot for storage, bouncing through and over potholes, splashing mud everywhere, and generally being miserable.

We did what we could to make it easier for him. We had the dirt lot covered in fresh, compacted gravel. I bought Terry a waterproof jacket to wear over his normal jacket to keep the rain from soaking in. We kept the pot of coffee fresh and the offices warm so that he could retreat. Terry was a great employee who rode a bike to work on most days and had his wife pick him up for the trip home. He was also probably the most normal of us all.

Others

We had a semi-regular crew of day laborers who came in and threw boxes for us. On days when we did not have anything to throw, we often hired them for side jobs like painting and landscaping.

If Obi-Wan from *Star Wars: A New Hope* had walked into the warehouse, he would have said, "You'll never find a more wretched hive of scum and villainy." I am joking, of course. These people complemented me. They provided strength to help with my weaknesses.

Bad Employees Do Not Exist

You might disagree with the subheading above. There are employees who steal, for example, but are they bad? I am not a moral relativist. Stealing is wrong, period. But I have learned that there is no such thing as a good human or a bad human. If we think about ourselves honestly, we discover that we have our own problems, just like our employees. The real question is whether our employees are the best fit for our needs.

As mentioned at the beginning of the book, Chester and I could not housebreak Mutt. We would catch him peeing off the dock and then yell at him to use the restroom. He would stop for a couple of months, but eventually we'd hear from someone that he was at it again.

I finally whined at Chester and said, "He's your friend. Can't you get him to stop?"

Chester threw up his hands. "I've tried. I've known him for forty years and he's not going to change. Fire him if you want to."

I did not fire him. Mutt was not housebroken. He was in his seventies, so I figured that he either had bad bladder control or a wicked sense of humor. The former was pure speculation but the latter was obvious. It seems funny, but I miss those days when we tried to potty train a septuagenarian who was apparently experiencing his second childhood. Was Mutt a bad employee? To the contrary.

We had a forklift driver who was supposed to temporarily substitute for Mutt while he took the winter off at his second home in Southern California. The replacement had been part of our day labor crew. When we found out that he had forklift skills, we gave him an extended tryout for a permanent position.

He was a great guy with a good attitude and who always showed up to work on time. But he lacked the sense of urgency and energy we needed. The nature of our work required forklift operators to constantly jump off the machine to check the position of the forks in relation to the diverse types of freight, pallets, and crates. Otherwise, the product could easily be damaged.

Mutt's replacement could not hack it. He never wanted to get off the forklift, which greatly increased the risk of damaging expensive products. Chester explained to him what we needed many times over weeks, but the guy either could not or would not cooperate.

Mutt surprised us by returning from his Southern California vacation weeks earlier than anticipated. So, we stopped calling his replacement and put Mutt back to work. The replacement was a good guy and a good forklift operator. He simply was not the right fit. He ended up going back to a refrigerated warehouse where he had worked before.

Motivation

We covered this. Money is the motivation.

Coaching Employees

Katie informed me that I am required to write more about motivation. I have been properly coached.

Motivation II

According to a 2019 PR Newswire report, 57 percent of all workers leave their jobs because they dislike their managers. An additional 32 percent considered leaving their jobs because of their managers. The remaining 12 percent of employees have never considered leaving their companies. Somehow that equals 101 percent of the respondents. I am not sure how that works. Whatever the case, 89 percent of the respondents either quit their jobs or considered quitting because of their bosses. This means that startup owners are squarely in the crosshairs. So, I recommend that you figure out what kind of leader you want to be and then treat people how you would want to be treated . . . and be sure to listen to feedback.

The same study found that people were primarily motivated by wanting to make a difference in the world. Money was less important. I suspect that most employees want to make a difference in the world by having more money—so that they can eat, have a roof over their heads, and maybe raise a couple of kids. Money is at the top of the employees' hierarchy of needs. Once you have that base covered, other things, such as "making a difference," become possible.

I might not be the best guide on this topic. I started my corporate career working for a Fortune 500 company. As the years went on, I proceeded to get jobs with smaller and smaller companies. Then, as a startup owner, I literally worked for myself while writing about how I used to do things. I moved on from my other jobs in part because I wanted to gain new skills, challenge myself, and grow in responsibility. As for my fourth job (running Joel's Warehouse), I'm not sure if I fired myself or quit, but I can confirm my boss was a jerk.

I'm not going to delve into recent management theory about motivation, but as required by Katie, I will elaborate on a few ideas. First, I think we all realize that work sucks. No one would do it if they were not paid. Second, it is appropriate to acknowledge that workers need money to survive. Third, unless the company is successful, there won't be any money to pay the employees. Fourth, employees need to help the company succeed so that they can get paid. Fifth, the boss or owner of the company should not try to make the workplace a pain in the ass. Otherwise, the boss will forever watch employees circulate through a rotating door, and that will doom productivity and lead to the company's demise. The end.

I admit that this is a simplistic view. I'm sure that HR and management staff at multinational corporations would complain that I don't understand the complexity of employee-employer relations. That could also explain why I don't work at a multinational corporation. However, I would like to see a study in which employees are given a choice between having one paid day per month off to plant trees or a $10,000 annual salary increase. I suspect that 99 percent of the employees would pick the latter.

How did we do it at Joel's Warehouse? We paid more up front for quality forklift operators. As the company became financially successful, we provided an end-of-year bonus to thank everyone for their hard work. We did not act like assholes to our employees. In fact, we tried to be as flexible as we could while getting the work done. We were honest about our expectations and the goals of the company.

All this seems basic, but many companies do not act like that. I know from experience. Some companies are not even honest with themselves, much less with their employees. When you see a company announce mass layoffs at the same time the CEOs are getting multimillion-dollar bonuses, you naturally question the morals and ethics of those folks. This is not just a private sector trend. As I write, we're still in the middle of the Covid-19 pandemic. Numerous public officials have declared lockdowns and then immediately disregarded those lockdowns.

Company Culture

You would think that companies would simply want employees to show up and do their jobs well. Based on my experience, that is not always the case. Anyone who has started a new job has also faced the challenge of trying to fit in relationally. Workplaces are, in many respects, like high schools. They are full of cliques, gossip, and people who do not wash their damn hands after using the bathroom.

Managers who are sensitive about company culture talk about "team dynamics" when they hire. That makes sense to me. The last thing anyone wants is to lower the performance of an entire team because the new hire does not click with the twenty-year company veteran. Also, no one wants a team of nonconfrontational, low-expectation, bland and boring personalities.

I am not an expert in corporate cultures. I do not have a Ph.D. in corporate psychology or human interfacing in diametric tribes. I am not even sure if those are real things. But I was good at running my own warehousing company. I knew my company inside and out. I became an expert in operating a warehouse.

We built a culture at Joel's Warehouse. We believed in an all-hands-on-deck work ethic. We shared and listened to ideas. We all reaped the rewards of our hard work. There was zero bureaucracy, no time for office politics, and no tolerance for blowing smoke up asses. It was a place where we tried to make it trouble-free for clients to do business with us. We strove to be courteous, efficient, and communicative. We all worked together for mutual benefits.

Our culture was deliberate and intentional. It was not an accident, and the work was never finished. At no point did we think we had reached perfection. We constantly reminded ourselves of the standards we were trying to uphold. At our small business, every employee had a significant impact on the company culture.

As the owner of your startup, you will have a huge amount of influence over your company's culture. Developing that culture is a central function of the organization, just like IT and HR. It will permeate everything you do, so you should give it a great deal of consideration. Here are some helpful steps to think about as you proceed.

Step 1: Model the Behavior You Want from Others

My oldest child, Aedan, gets a regular dose of this lesson. He and his younger brother, Brennan, are responsible for getting ready for bed, and if they fail to get ready in a reasonable amount of time, Aedan loses privileges first. If the ruckus continues after Aedan loses his privileges, then the youngest kid loses his privileges too. Aedan does not think this is fair. He is right. Most of the time, we treat each kid according to their own behaviors. Aedan doesn't get punished because Brennan decided to write on a wall with a pen. However, it's also true that Aedan, as the oldest, needs to learn what it means to be a responsible leader. I have a couple of reasons for this thinking.

First, if Aedan doesn't participate in bedtime upheaval, his brother won't goof off for long. The energy that causes the bedtime disruption requires both kids. Second, I want my oldest to model the proper behavior for his younger brother. My oldest needs to understand that his younger brother will take cues from what he sees his older brother doing.

I believe these same dynamics play a role in forming company cultures, especially in a startup where the owner is the most visible person. If you (the owner) consider workplace gossip to be unproductive and contrary to your ideal culture, then you should not participate in it. Neither should your managers. They should encourage their employees to not participate in gossip. Hypocrisy is a quick way to lose credibility.

Step 2: Set Reasonable Expectations

Everyone is a participant in creating the company culture, and so everyone should be an advocate for maintaining the standard. Chester and I set the standard from the beginning and our employees took their cues from that. We reinforced the company culture by telling our employees what we expected from them. If we saw an interaction we did not like, we intervened as needed. At the very least, we discussed the issue with the employee. Everyone knew the expectations and knew they would be reinforced.

Step 3: Own Your Mistakes

You are not perfect. When you make mistakes, own them and move on. It doesn't diminish you as a person to admit your errors. It won't lessen you in the eyes of your employees. If anything, owning the mistakes should increase the respect that your employees have for you. Hold yourself to the same standard as everyone else—or even to a higher standard.

People Are the Culture

Dealing with other people is never simple. But it is important to hire the people who fit well within your company culture and who are eager to contribute. You should have a clear understanding of who you need to fill each role, and who will be part of your inner circle. Listen to everyone before you make a big decision. If someone is not a good fit, or worse, you should find a way to cut ties. Let them find an employer and position that is better suited to them. It will be better for you and better for them.

7

Competitor Relationships

As you think about your competitors, several thoughts might run through your head. *We're going to kick those guys' butts. Their product sucks. Their sales tactics are shady. Maybe they'll hire me some day.* Meanwhile, government employees never think about competitors. They never even use the word. Rather, they think about ways to tax businesses.

Then there are business leaders who look for ways to *collude* with competitors at the expense of customers. Did someone say "price fixing"? Those people often end up in prison.

In my little corner of the world, the warehouses located near Joel's Warehouse could either be competitors, vendors, or customers. On extremely hectic days, they could be all three. We *never* discussed price fixing or conspired to raise prices against customers, or anything of the like. However, there were some interesting scenarios.

Competitors As Competitors

Remember the customer mentioned earlier who handled paper rolls? We bid for that business every year, even though I knew that a warehouse nearby always handled that product. I lost the bid every year because we were not set up to handle the product and therefore had to increase our bid price.

We ran into this situation all the time when bidding on business. Customers asked several warehouses for prices, and then they picked the winner based on the combination of price and service. Standard competitive stuff. Hooray free market!

We had three advantages: We were small, we had a ramp leading out of the warehouse, and we were small. Being small was an advantage because some customers really hated to be forced to use a vendor's system. They preferred to dictate the systems that would be used. For example, if XYZ mattress company wanted Joel's Warehouse to send spreadsheets every day with updated inventory counts, then Joel's Warehouse would do that. If Amazon required XYZ mattress company to use Amazon's appointment system for deliveries to Amazon's warehouse, then XYZ mattress company would use Amazon's appointment system. Who decides these terms usually depends on which company has the highest net worth.

A brief word to tech savvy readers. I know electronic data interchange (EDI) is a thing. However, small business owners don't want to pay someone to program the EDI for us. At Joel's Warehouse we didn't have a WMS (warehouse management system) anyway. We were quite content (ahem) to do what we were told by the larger corporations with which we did business. Our customers simply wanted clear, timely, and accurate communication. *How* this was accomplished was usually not that important, as long as the work got done. Phone calls, emails, text messages, spreadsheets—it didn't matter as long as communication was timely and coherent.

So, when XYZ mattress company eventually found Joel's Warehouse, we would be so grateful for the business that we would do whatever they wanted. We could win the business of any company that wanted to bully us. Chester was known to like punishment, so it was a win-win.

Another advantage of being small was that competitors never noticed us. Elephants don't notice ants.

Competitors As Customers

The old adage "when it rains it pours" applies well to the warehousing business. When we were full, more freight was always on the way.

"Ten more loads coming in, Chester," I'd warn as forklifts raced around.

Chester would look around at the stacks of supersacks and pallets. "We'll stick 'em on the roof!" he'd yell over his shoulder.

"Also, six loads of crates coming in," I'd tell Chester.

"Can they go outside?" he'd ask.

"Nope, but they'll start picking them up first thing in the morning."

"I'll get the warehouse stretcher," Chester would joke.

Sometimes space got so tight in the warehouse that we could barely turn the forklifts around. Somehow, we always made everything fit.

On many occasions, our competitors became customers because their warehouses would get too full. They would take pity on us and ask us to store their overflow freight. On other occasions, our competitors would be too busy to remove their containers from the port, and so they would ask us to help with some "power." We didn't have any trucks, but we did have a lot of friends with trucks. We would make $50 per container by brokering some of the moves out of the port.

Chester enjoyed the brokering work more than anything else we did. "Think of it," Chester would say. "We get paid, and someone else does all the work!"

I countered that people with physical assets like warehouses and trucks were hard to replace, while a phone jockey was not. "Sometimes it's more important *who* you know," Chester replied. "You don't need a warehouse or truck as long as you know people who do." As a result, Chester spent more time on his phone than a teenage girl with a new crush.

In some cases, we had equipment that our competitors did not have, such as our forklift called the Beast. It had a sufficiently low profile that it could fit inside a container. One competitor/vendor/customer brought over a bunch of crates of wallboard, which we unloaded from a flatbed. However, that company could not stack the crates and push them into the container with their standard warehouse lifts. The Beast had no problem doing this. As a result, it was sometimes called the Sexy Beast.

The biggest problem with having competitors as customers is that we knew they were making a profit beyond what they paid us. That hurt. If they offered us 80 cents per square foot to store something, we knew they were getting at least $1 per square foot from their customer.

There is the usually unspoken and sometimes spoken rule of not back-soliciting the business. For example, if Big Warehouse gave us five thousand square feet of product to store for Big Box Inc., we were not supposed to go to Big Box Inc. and say, "Why not cut out the middleman and use us directly?" We could do practically whatever we wanted to our competitors and it would be considered a normal part of doing business. But if we back solicited, we would quickly find ourselves with no friends and a suffering business.

So, remember this as you grow your startup: Competitors aren't just competitors; they're also vendors.

Competitors As Vendors

In the warehousing business, it is almost impossible to be all things to all customers. At our peak, we operated five forklifts. Occasionally, we would temporarily lease other forklifts to deal with a specific project. We also had a couple of pallet jacks for day laborers to use when they palletized hand-stacked boxes.

Every forklift has unique characteristics, which enables them to handle different types of products and loads. The drivers do best if they know the exact specs. One of our forklifts was too tall to fit inside a container. Due to lack of space in the warehouse, it often had to stay outside. It was a big machine with seventy-two-inch forks that we used to load and unload flatbed trailers of lumber. The Beast was good for certain types of work, whereas the Tank and the Speedboat were good for other jobs.

As a result of our equipment limitations, we could not do certain types of work. But we wanted to be a one-stop shop for our customers. For this reason, we had to be friendly with our competitors. We knew that we might need to use their strengths to cover for our weaknesses.

For example, one of our customers imported bundles of steel pipe. They worked with a consignee who did not have a dock, which meant that they needed the pipe to be transferred to a flatbed. Our role was to pull the pipe out of the containers, run them down our ramp, and then load them onto a flatbed.

Unloading the first several containers went smoothly. The pipe was in twenty-foot sections, and each bundle weighed about five thousand pounds. We had a "carpet pick" attachment for the forklifts that we used to strap each bundle of pipe. We would then lift the pipe and back out of the container. It was important to raise the pipe bundle and not drag them to avoid damage.

When the customer said they had another twenty-five containers coming in, I was excited for the chance to handle them. The customer claimed that they were "just like the first ones." A week later we brought the first container over from the port and realized that these pipes were not like the first ones. The bundles were thirty feet long, so our "carpet pick" wasn't long enough to lift the far end of the bundles. This meant we would need to drag them out of the containers. In addition, we no longer had an easy way to get them out of the warehouse. They were too long for the garage door and the ramp. Creative ideas emerged, such as using multiple forklifts, but they all implied a time-consuming operation.

We believed that a friend nearby could help us do the work. He didn't have a warehouse, but he specialized in heavy lifts of between fifty thousand and 120,000 pounds. We sent one container to him, which he managed easily. However, he didn't want to do the other twenty-four containers because he was too busy. That hurt.

We went to another friend who also had the right equipment, but he was a competitor on the warehouse side of things. Little Jimmy had been one of his customers. The guy agreed to do the port drayage and to empty the containers for us. We haggled over prices, but he eventually completed the job.

These factors and others cut into our profits. At the end of the day, we made $300 on a total invoice of around $50,000. I wrote a check for $49,700 to our competitor. I was relieved that it worked out as well as it did.

A couple of months later, the same customer called me and offered us another twenty loads. Here is the basic transcript of the call.

"We don't want to do those anymore," I replied. "Here's my competitor's phone number. They know how to handle your business."

"Can we still call you for other containers?"

"Yes, just not the bundles of pipe."

I never heard from the customer again. That was fine because we knew our capabilities and limitations. And we knew the same about our competitors. This leads me to the next point.

Competitors As Allies

A competitor can also be an ally, helping to establish three important types of business: base accounts, regular accounts, and project accounts.

In the freight world, everyone I know has a "base account" or two. These accounts make up the steady daily routine of the business. They often contribute at least half of the company's revenue. A large warehouse might have a well-known base account, such as Walmart, Target, or Best Buy. To expand a large operation, the companies often lease four or five warehouses within a fifteen-minute drive of each other.

Little Jimmy, with his supersacks, served as our original base account. Later we added a lumber base account. In our third year, the XYZ mattress company would provide more revenue than Little Jimmy. Unfortunately, due to some problems with Amazon, they had to shift their warehousing needs from the coast to the center of the country. Suddenly, they were gone.

I approached a large warehousing company (warehouse

A) that was located next to their competitor (warehouse B). I hoped that warehouse A could become our ally. I toured their facility and asked if they wanted to get rid of any accounts. I saw no point in being shy or too proud to ask. The answer was yes. Warehouse A wanted to get rid of some accounts with types of business that Joel's Warehouse could handle. They were happy to get rid of accounts because they had just established the base account of warehouse B. Warehouse A had no capacity to serve the account, so it was paying warehouse B to do that work. What a tangled web we weave!

Competitors can also help to establish regular accounts, which provide steady business. Individually, they never generate more than a small percent of overall revenue. However, collectively, they can produce significant revenue, perhaps even rivalling the base account. We had about twenty regular accounts. Their needs were more generic, and they often moved from warehouse to warehouse in search of lower costs. As a result, some of our competitors pushed them toward Joel's Warehouse.

Then there are project accounts, such as the bundled pipe account I mentioned above. These companies might call every couple of months with a hot twenty loads and then not call again for weeks, or ever again. One of our competitors became an ally when a nearby barbeque grill distributor mistakenly added an extra zero to the number of grills they had ordered from China. The grill distributor's warehouse quickly ran out of room, so they sought space at our competitor's facility, who also did not have room. The competitor referred the work to us. For three months we filled our second warehouse with thousands of grills. When that project was over, we never heard from the distributor again.

All of this was standard practice between us and our competitors (allies). Everyone knew they could not do everything alone. Our primary goal was to make sure we served the customers.

Wretched Cow Hides and Bad Karma

Sometimes relationships with our competitors seemed like an exchange of bad karma.

I took a phone call one day from Bob over at port terminal 69. He had a problem with a damaged container. My competitor, Chuck at Big Warehouse, told Bob that we could handle it. Chuck and I regularly sent each other business. His Big Warehouse specialized in rail freight, so I sent him all the rail requests that I received. Everyone was happy.

"We damaged a container trying to lift it." Bob explained. "The freight is palletized; we just need it swapped into a good container and we'll call it good."

"What's the freight and pallet size?"

"Cowhides, standard pallets."

Cowhides? I'd never done those before. I quoted Bob a price for the transload, the pickup at the port, and the delivery back to the port. He said the price was good.

We sent a driver into terminal 69 and picked up the damaged container filled with cowhides. We then then sent him back to get an empty container that would house the hides. While the driver was gone, we opened the doors of the damaged container and recoiled in shock.

Three days prior, these cowhides had covered live beasts saying moo and eating grass in a field. Now they were piled on pallets and baking inside the container. Even on a cool but sunny day, it is not unusual for the temperature inside a container to rise above one hundred degrees. The day we received the hides, it was sunny and warm. The smell of cowhides slowly cooking inside the container was potent.

Something else concerned us. Plastic lined the bottom of the container and stretched four feet up each wall. It was all secured with ropes to various tie-down points. We weren't sure what that meant, but it seemed ominous. When we cut the ropes at the entryway of the container, the plastic fell. Suddenly, two feet of cowhide "sweat" poured out of the container. The liquid was brownish, smelled horrible, and looked like it would stain anything.

"I've got to go buy some tarps," Chester mumbled, running away from the smell.

When he returned, we placed tarps everywhere the forklift would be needed. We set out to transload the hides from one container to the other. In the places where drops of cowhide sweat missed the tarps and hit the warehouse floor, the stain lingered for months.

I called Bob at terminal 69 and told him he would need to pay for the tarps, including those we used to line the new container. He readily agreed, but I could sense that Bob knew a thing or two about the cowhide containers. I suspect Chuck at Big Warehouse knew about cowhides too, which is probably why he turned down the job in the first place.

However, what goes around comes around, even if it is unintentional. Bad karma is like that. Bob from terminal 69 called again to say he had another damaged container filled with bundles of recycled paper. He wanted us to unload it and reload it into a new container.

I knew a few things about bundles of recycled paper, enough to know that we didn't want anything to do with it. I envisioned our staff cleaning paper scrap out of our warehouse for weeks. I could imagine the baling straps breaking and our staff figuring out how to bundle the paper again. Our neighbor specialized in bundling recycled paper and then shipping it to China for processing. So, I told Bob to call those guys.

A couple of hours later, I looked out my office window and saw the container of recycled paper sitting at our neighbor's warehouse yard, engulfed in flames. My neighbor proceeded to use a torch to cut open the side of the container while one of his guys sprayed water into the container. The more they cut apart the container, the more the fire spread inside.

As I found out later, the container roof had somehow caved in at the terminal. Thus, he could not drive the forklift into the container to unload the freight. The terminal workers gave him permission to cut the side off so he could remove the paper bundles. When someone uses a cutting torch to open the side of a container filled with paper, the odds are quite high that a fire will start. Once it started, they had no choice but to keep cutting so that they could spray water in from the side. A couple of hours later there was nothing left but a charred, wet, twisted metal shell. Our neighbor jokingly blamed me for everything because I had referred the customer to him.

Like I said, bad karma among competitors has a way of going around.

8

Vendor Relationships

Vendors, with whom you must have good relations, want three things from you: pay your bills on time, don't abuse their products, and do not be a jerk. In my experience, some people struggle most with the don't-be-a-jerk part.

Don't Be a Jerk

Let's say that your startup is a restaurant. You've been in business for a few months and things are going well. However, one night a customer comes in who gets drunk and belligerent. He makes rude comments to the waitress and leaves her a $2 tip on a $100 tab. The guy was a jerk. Chances are rare you will even see this guy again, but he's put you in a bad mood.

Then the bread delivery is late, for the third week in a row. The delay makes it hard for you to serve bread to lunch customers. The delivery driver is apologetic and polite, but because you are in a bad mood, you take it out on the driver anyway.

The next week the bread arrives late again. Due to the

previous delay, you had to temporarily suspend lunch orders because you didn't have enough hamburger buns for your locally famous patty melt. You angrily reprimand the driver again as he wordlessly finishes his delivery.

Then you get a call from his supervisor, who tells you to find a new bread company. You are in shock. You apologize profusely, but he tells you that the company won't work with clients who abuse their drivers. It's over.

You make some calls and find out that the competing bread company is willing to do the deliveries, but they can't start for two weeks. Their product is not the same and it costs 15 percent more. Your regular customers will notice the lower bread quality, which means they might not come back. Your profit margins have become narrower and you will need to buy bread from a grocery store to fill in the two-week gap.

Why are you suffering? Take a long, hard look in the mirror. Then look at your employees who depend on you to feed themselves and their families. As a small business owner, you cannot afford to lose sight of them because of a late delivery trucker who might have also had a bad day.

Don't be a jerk to your vendors. In fact, don't be a jerk to anyone. There are times you need to be a jerk, but in those cases be a *principled* jerk, such as when you need to expel a drunk and belligerent customer who has harassed your waitress. In this scenario, you would be protecting your staff and setting a boundary for appropriate behavior in your establishment. You would not, in fact, be a jerk; you would be exerting your right to enforce rules on your premises. You would be a leader.

To lead a successful startup, you need vendors to help you. They won't hold your hand unless you are kind to them. The opposite of being a jerk is to show people mercy or grace. As I started my warehousing business, the most expensive and difficult step was to find warehouse space. Most real estate owners wanted at least a five-year term. And most of them would not trust a random dude with a startup company to pay $13,000 per month in rent. That landlord took a chance on us, and for that chance we worked diligently to show we deserved it.

Chester and I looked at a lot of warehouses. Some landlords wouldn't even talk to us. Other landlords wanted two years rent up front. Some wanted ten-year contracts. Some were willing to lease to us if we were willing to assume one hundred thousand square feet, at a cost of roughly $65,000 per month. We were lucky to find twenty-five thousand square feet for $13,000 per month.

At Joel's Warehouse, we always paid our rent on time. By gaining trust, we eventually expanded to sixty-five thousand square feet spread across two warehouses, both owned by the same landlord. Then, before we left, we used our connections to find two occupants for him, one for each warehouse. The landlord never had to go without steady rental income, and we left everything in better shape than when he leased it to us.

Treat vendors right and eventually . . .

Vendors Will Save Your Bacon

If your customer is successful, then you will be successful. Remember that when you are dealing with your customers; to them, you're a vendor. This is especially true if you're in a business-to-business environment like our warehouse.

As Little Jimmy's vendor, we had the potential of screwing up his relationships with his customers, which could have cost him a huge amount of business. He entrusted us with his livelihood, and we took that seriously. If we helped him to be successful, then his gains would benefit us.

We could not operate our warehouse without forklifts, so our second favorite vendor (after our landlord) was the company that supplied us with forklifts. When the Beast, for example, was out of commission, our operation came to a complete standstill. We would potentially miss deadlines related to our customers' ship departures, container free-time expirations, and other demands. A sick forklift could seriously disrupt the rhythm and flow of moving freight in and out of the warehouse.

Once when the Beast broke, we called our forklift vendor and begged for a mechanic or a loaner forklift. We had leased forklifts from this vendor for years, and we had purchased the Beast and the Tank from him. We paid every bill on time. We were polite. And now . . . we conveyed our urgent need for help.

It was a Friday. He agreed to send the mechanic over the next morning so that we could be up and running on Monday, even though his mechanics normally didn't work weekends.

He could have easily sent the mechanic the following week, but he understood that would disrupt our deadlines. That's the kind of relationship you want with all your vendors.

During another business crisis, a competitor became a vendor who helped us rescue Little Jimmy.

"Uh, we have a problem," said Little Jimmy's nephew when I answered the phone. Little Jimmy's nephew frequently called to say there was a problem, but the problem was often minor.

"What's up?" I asked.

"There is a ship arriving in one week with fifty loads in it, and another coming the week after that with another fifty loads."

This time there was a *problem*. It was Monday morning of Thanksgiving week. Our warehouse was full. Little Jimmy was out of town on vacation in Mexico. His nephew had no idea what to do next. A disaster in the making.

The root of the problem was easy to see. Little Jimmy's biggest customer did not inform him about the incoming freight with enough lead time. No warehouse would have room for a hundred containers of unannounced freight.

Knowing the root cause of the situation did not matter at this point. We just needed to figure out a solution. I called my realtor and hoped that he would have an idea. He did, and it was better than I had hoped. Due to complicated legal and financial matters, there was an empty warehouse a few miles from us.

I had, over the years, been a vendor to and competitor of the owners of that warehouse. I had also been a coworker with the owner's daughter-in-law. They knew me and we had numerous business relationships in common. Now I hoped to become their customer, to lease their warehouse space for three months so that I could handle the one hundred loads. I knew that most landlords would immediately reject this type of short-term arrangement. But because of our long-standing relationship, and because we had the same realtor, we got the deal done just before Thanksgiving. The ship arrived the next Monday.

It was a miracle. For warehouse space to be available at all was rare. And to find space owned by someone willing to help us was difficult to comprehend.

Other Vendors

As you establish your startup, you should avoid relying on just one vendor. We loved our forklift provider, but he couldn't do everything we needed. We built some other relationships and went through three other bad vendors before finding someone reasonable. There is such a thing as a bad vendor, which is why you should have more than one.

When we temporarily needed to rent a squeeze-clamp forklift, another vendor quickly delivered a model. However, it did not work for our needs. Later that day, we called the vendor and asked them to retrieve the machine. They picked it up the next morning, but then they billed us $1300 for the rental, as though we had kept it for a month.

I called the sales rep, but never got a resolution. Their policy was set in stone. He never called me back. Then he stopped answering my calls or responding to my emails. No one else at the company would help me either. After two months of constant harassment from them about paying the invoice, I paid the bill and moved on with life. I also vowed to never use them again. They won the battle but lost the war.

We found another company that could offer the right type of forklift. They were courteous, understood what we needed, and were responsive—everything we could ask for in a vendor. Had we needed to switch from our primary vendor, we would have given them all our business. They got our secondary forklift business from there on out.

Cultivating multiple vendors also helped us keep their prices in check. One vendor seemed to increase his prices the more we used him. In any given month, he would first charge us $400 to transload a shipment and then he would charge us $650 for the tenth load. Meanwhile I was trying to provide consistent prices to my customers, and I did not want to convey that I was pulling rates out of my hat.

To combat his price increases, we cultivated a relationship with another heavy lift vendor who would give us a consistent price of $500, day in and day out. We started using our primary vendor until his price creeped up. Then we'd switch to the other vendor. After a couple of weeks, our primary vendor would ask why we had stopped sending freight to him. I was frank and told him that his price had become too high. He promised to do better, but the same pattern continued.

For these reasons, and others, it made sense for us to have back-up vendors. I recommend it for any startup. Never put all your eggs in one basket.

Side Hustle

Our vendors also provided us an opportunity to generate money. For example, we were able to build a profitable relationship with a pallet vendor. Providing pallets to customers is part of the warehousing business. When we had a container come in from overseas with twelve hundred floor-loaded boxes, we would palletize and shrink wrap the product.

We received thousands of pallets every year from overseas shippers. However, domestic shippers did not want them because the standard pallet size for overseas shipping is different than the size needed for continental US shipping (CONUS). As a result, we had to purchase a ton of domestic pallets while also getting stuck with thousands of overseas pallets that we couldn't get rid of.

Thankfully, our pallet vendor was willing to take many overseas pallets off our hands for free. He broke them apart and repurposed the wood. Sometimes, when the planets lined up, a customer would ask to buy some of our overseas pallets for specific loading purposes. In those cases, we made a few more bucks than usual. God bless those customers.

9

Operations

You have probably heard the saying, "You don't want to know how sausage is made." That might be true for you in relation to this chapter. But I recommend learning how the sausage is made. This chapter will give you an inside look at warehousing operations, which are, as we all now know due to the pandemic, essential for everything in life. Warehousing enables you to have food, electronics, and medical supplies. And even if your startup is not a warehouse business, this chapter will emphasize the importance of your own operations.

Prior to running my own warehouses, I had always worked in a corporate office, far from the action. All corporate offices, regardless of the industry, are basically the same. Workers slog through endless meetings pretending to run the companies from little cubicles. These business professionals might be a little big-headed. They talk about "being at corporate" and having "corner offices" and think that "keeping their hands clean" is something to be proud of. I liked to remind people that the real work was happening elsewhere and to have a little humility. At best, employees in a corporate office are working in a support role for the people who do the important operations work. In operations, theory meets reality. A successful startup will depend on quality operations, even if it is a dirty job.

Dirty Jobs

Mike Rowe, host of "Dirty Jobs," is one of my favorite TV personalities. I think he understands the importance of operations, that the real work is happening somewhere outside the cubicles.

I enjoyed the fact that my office was in the warehouse, and that the forklifts were never more than a few feet away. I could see the operations through my office window. Most days I spent time on the forklift, when we were shorthanded, or when staff members were on break, or when I wanted to have my hands on the operation. There were times when I had to jump on the forklift after making sales calls while wearing a suit and tie, just to finish unloading a container. I climbed on freight and got covered in dirt and dust. I threw boxes and got covered in sweat. I had a dozen other things on my plate, but nothing was as important as operations.

Chester was our ultimate dirty jobs guy at the beginning. As the smallest guy on our three-man crew he, at age seventy-two, could squeeze into the tight spots. He once entered a vehicle through the sunroof so that he could steer it while we dragged it out of a container with a forklift. He once climbed between bundles of lumber and a container ceiling, an eighteen-inch gap, because he forgot what he had loaded.

He ran security camera cable through the warehouse rafters. You know what happens when you disturb thirty years of dust on rafters? You get dirty. As I drove the forklift, black dirt and dust rained down on me as he positioned the wire. This was what we did for fun on a Saturday morning.

Eventually, Juan Carlos joined our crew as the new dirty jobs guy, which made Chester "happier than a pig in shit."

We never lost sight of the fact that our primary goal was to take care of our customers. That ultimately came down to operations. Our employees knew that taking care of operations meant that some jobs would be dirty and hard. We often had to find creative solutions to problems, but we always kept safety first.

Safety

The freight is heavy. Forklifts are large and dangerous. Combine freight and a forklift and . . . well, we had to emphasize safety.

We established good habits, such as setting the emergency brake when we jumped off one of the bulls. Nevertheless, I still saw forklift operators jump off a forklift, accidentally bump the directional lever, and then chase the runaway machine. These bulls don't move fast, but they weigh several tons and have large metal lances on them. So, even at a slow speed they can destroy things and run people over.

Like raising children, I found myself repeatedly coaching forklift drivers in the same behaviors. Unlike raising children, the forklift drivers should have known better already. They did, in fact, know; however, sometimes they were so focused on getting a job done that they would forget a step.

For example, imagine a driver who is unloading pallets of soup from a trailer. While fighting to get the fork underneath a pallet, he hits an obstruction. He's in a hurry. There are twenty more pallets to unload, and a trailer or two waiting. He has a couple of options: push on through and potentially damage the freight or get off the forklift and look for the obstruction.

The proper procedure would be to set the parking brake, jump off the forklift, and look for the problem. There might simply be an out-of-place cross member in the pallet, in which case he would just need to reposition the fork. If he's unlucky, he might find that the pallet broke and that there are cans of soup on the floor. Depending on how bad it is, the whole pallet might need to be unstacked by hand and restacked onto a better pallet.

The stakes are high. If he decides to jump off the bull without setting the parking brake, he might find himself crushed between the forklift and the soup. If he survives and escapes without injury, then people would make fun of him for the rest of his warehousing career. If he dies, it would be a tragedy. At least his story would be told to the next generation of forklift operators in hopes of helping them to avoid the same mistake. In fact, I knew one guy (at a prior operation) who wasn't paying attention and drove his forklift right off a dock. The story was endlessly repeated because he didn't get seriously injured. He became a "legend" in the industry, but for all the wrong reasons.

My warehouse offices have had views of neighboring operations, which enabled me to see some interesting things. I watched as a guy unloaded a short flatbed truck. As he was backing off the flatbed with the last pallet, the truck driver pulled away from the dock. For a moment, the forklift was suspended between the dock and the trailer. Then it tumbled over, landing upside down. The forklift driver was able to walk away because, thankfully, engineers have designed forklifts with protective cages that can withstand the weight of an upside-down lift.

At Joel's Warehouse, safety was everyone's responsibility. It took more than just management-led training programs. I expected employees to hold each other accountable. If someone wasn't setting the parking brake, the other staff were supposed to offer a reminder. If people were in the warehouse without reflective safety vests, a staff member was supposed to bring them vests. If any of us saw any unsafe behavior, we were called to intervene, report it, or do whatever was necessary to prevent an accident.

Sometimes getting the job done is complicated.

Getting the Job Done

When we were still willing to unload cars from containers, we had a customer who imported unique models from Germany. Much like the Aussie's cars, these German cars could not typically be found in the US. We first received from him a twenty-foot container with two small vehicles in it.

Someone used creative engineering to fit both cars into the container. The first one had been backed in. The nose of the car had been lifted until it almost touched the container's ceiling. The front had been supported by lumber struts and a crossbeam placed underneath the wheels. The second car had been driven in nose first, positioned underneath the first car, and then blocked and braced so that it would not roll.

We had mini sledgehammers that would suffice to remove the lower car's blocking and bracing. We then removed that car from the container without difficulty. Then we stared aghast at the elevated car. How exactly would we get this car down?

In such scenarios, ideas are suggested and then rejected one by one. We couldn't stick the forks underneath the car because the underside of the vehicle would get torn up. We also couldn't get our forks that high because the guard on the back of the forks would hit the container's ceiling. And then we realized that the crossbeam underneath the tires was secured to the lumber struts with railroad spikes. A mini sledgehammer would not get the job done.

Mutt and I wrangled over the problem for a while until finally we came up with a plan. Step one was to buy a chainsaw. Then we stacked pallets on the end of the forklift's forks and added many layers of cardboard to create a cushion. We then raised the forks as high as possible under the front of the vehicle. I started up the chainsaw and cut through each end of the crossbeam. The car then settled on the stacked pallets and cardboard.

Mutt slowly lowered the car as far as he could, but we forgot to account for the vehicle's ground clearance. The height of the pallets and cardboard was so tall that when the forks hit the ground, the car's front tires were still suspended eight inches off the ground. After further deliberation, we broke apart the pallets starting on the bottom of the stack. As the boards shattered to pieces, the car's wheels dropped to the container floor. We had managed, yet again, to get a car down on all four tires without damage. That type of operation would keep me awake all night. Chester called them "freight-mares."

We had a rule that only Chester or I would "make the sausage" if the job required an abnormal, high-risk procedure. As the company owners, we needed to own such risks. For example, some regular freight arrived on a flatbed truck with two large crates about ten-feet long, eight-feet wide, and eight-feet high. One large tarp was spread across both crates to protect them from the weather. Because of their size, we couldn't take both crates off at one time. It was raining, so we wanted to leave the tarp on.

Mutt used the forklift to raise me to the top of the crates so that I could crawl around and cut the tarp in half where the two crates abutted.

"What floor do you want to get off?" Mutt asked, as though he were operating an elevator in a department store. "Ladies' lingerie?"

Here I was, fourteen feet off the ground, crawling on my hands and knees, and wielding my knife against a tarp in the pouring rain. I was "living the dream."

Living the Dream?

That "living the dream" phrase has always bothered me. Frankly, people who use it usually need to find a new dream. I doubt that the over-the-road (OTR) truck drivers who tried to back their fifty-three-foot trailers up to our dock would say they were living the dream.

You would think that 100 percent of professional OTR drivers would be able to back into a loading dock without issue. However, truck drivers face the same problem that people in other professions face. Some surgeons have left a sponge inside a patient after a major surgery. Professional baseball pitchers can get the yips and forget how to throw a proper curve. And truck drivers sometimes can't align a trailer with a warehouse dock.

Some drivers are more experienced than others. I could always tell when there was going to be a problem by the look on the driver's face when I assigned a warehouse door. We would usually meet the arriving drivers in the yard, verify their identities, and then assign them a door. If the driver looked around the yard from one end to the other while his eyes anxiously shifted back and forth, I knew there was going to be a problem.

Usually, the driver would manage, after a few tries, to get the trailer properly backed up. Even if the trailer was a little crooked, we could still work with it. We could bridge gaps between the warehouse and trailer with dock plates, which could sustain ten thousand pounds of forklift and a couple thousand pounds of freight. But if Chester came into my office and invited me to "see something," I knew that a driver was having serious trouble.

On one such occasion, I arrived at the door and saw that our forklift operators were gathered at the door to watch. Mutt mumbled, "This is attempt number thirty-four." The driver started to back up the trailer again, but it quickly became clear that he was going to be a foot too far left. The driver pulled forward. "Thirty-five," Chester announced as the guy started backing up again. The outcome of this attempt was so bad that we could not get the dock plate to cover even half the trailer's entryway.

The driver, poor man, got out of the cab and came back to check.

"Fuck," he said while heading back to the cab.

"Thirty-six," said Chester as the driver tried again.

This time the outcome was that the dock plate could reach 60 percent of the trailer, a 10 percent improvement. The driver got out again and checked his positioning.

"Just fix the angle a little more and we'll make it work," Chester told the driver.

"Thirty-seven," Mutt said.

The driver finally got close enough for 80 percent of the dock plate to span the gap.

"Close enough," said Mutt as he jumped on the forklift.

Almost once a month, a new driver would arrive and compete for the Most Attempts to Back Up a Trailer award, which is one of the most prestigious awards in the warehouse industry.

Unlike operations space, we usually had more office space

than we could use. So, we often leased out space to trucking companies. They would often staff their office with two or three dispatchers. If we were lucky, one of the dispatchers also knew how to drive trucks. If a driver showed up with absolutely no chance of aligning a trailer with the dock, we could convince the dispatcher to do the job.

A long time ago, Chester would sometimes jump into truckers' cabs to help them back into a dock. He didn't have a commercial driver's license, but he had honed his skills using a yard hostler, which functions like a small version of a semi and is used to move containers at a warehouse or port. But while working for another company decades ago, Chester finally quit helping drivers. A husband-and-wife team drove into the yard where he was working. Chester hustled out to assign them a door. The truck had an extended sleeper cab for long trips. Chester climbed on the truck's step to talk to the driver, who had already opened the door. That was when the smell hit him: a blend of old, unwashed bodies, dirty sex stank, rotting garbage, and a hint of Eau de Poo de Pomeranian.

The smell hit him like a freight train barreling downhill. It knocked him off the truck step. He stumbled away and vomited in the bushes. Ever since, he refused to enter any truck cabs, even the ones occupied by drivers who desperately needed help to back up.

Regardless of your company's operations, being the owner has an advantage. I never had to get permission from anyone to implement our operations. I would confer about new ideas with Chester and the forklift drivers. Based on their feedback,

I would move forward to get the work done. For me, this was as close as I got to "living the dream." I no longer needed to wait for layers of approval to make changes, purchase things, or improve the business.

That said, it also meant that the business would suffer when I made mistakes. I had to be comfortable with that level of responsibility. This was never more apparent than when I was making decisions in the operations crucible.

The Crucible

I will say it again: Companies live and die by operations. Other functions are important and necessary, but leaders of successful companies remember that everything must support the operation.

I've met desk jockeys who think they can run companies via spreadsheets and KPIs (key performance indicators). All that is important, but somewhere there is a human being who is making the sausage. If that person is struggling, pencil whipping won't solve it.

The importance of operations often shows up in the news. We hear about employees complaining about long hours without breaks, or about employees working in unsafe conditions. You can bet that those people work in operations, not in human resources.

Angry customers typically don't yell at people in a company's purchasing department; they hunt for the operations manager. If the company is big enough to keep the operations staff away from the customers, then angry customers will yell at the customer service people who answer the phone. Eventually, the feedback might trickle over to the operations managers.

Operations staff also face the pressure of meeting crucial deadlines. News stories about video game developers have described how programmers are forced to work sixteen-hour days during the final weeks before the game is launched. Triple A video games can cost hundreds of millions of dollars to produce. After a release date is announced, the publisher will do everything possible to prevent a delay, which really means that the programmers pay the price.

For your startup, the pressure will be in operations. Being able to sell won't matter if you can't perform. That said, any startup will experience some operational kinks.

That's Kinky

All startup owners face a learning curve. We had some first-week jitters as we figured out the dock plate situation and learned how to unload and store supersacks when our first twenty-five containers arrived. Then we collected our thoughts, added needed equipment, and figured out how to receive the next thirty containers.

We worked out other kinks as well. For example, we bought chains and rigged them to our new dock plates. This made it easier to move them with a forklift from door to door without having to endure the loud, echoing clang of a dock plate falling on the floor. That sound made us cringe like a teenager seeing his first boob in a movie while seated next to his mom.

Chester discovered ways to speed up and simplify the process of unloading supersacks. We would unload two pallets from the container before setting the dock plate. Then, we found we could stack the bags in pyramid form, which freed up 30 percent of our floor space. We hoped that would lead to prosperity. In warehousing, space is money.

When the next thirty containers arrived, we set a goal of unloading ten per day. However, ports are unpredictable. A driver might spend all day in line and receive zero containers. By contrast, we had one driver who removed six containers in a day. The variance and uncertainty, which were maddening to customers, stemmed from numerous types of port disruptions: number of ships in rotation, a recently implemented operating system, labor disputes. One time a giant snake escaped and forced the terminal to shut down for two hours until animal control could capture it. Power outages, snow, accidents, fires, and a host of other events can cause ocean terminals to slow down. Remember that massive container ship that got stuck in the Suez Canal? Then there's that little thing called the Covid-19 pandemic, which has made supply chain issues apparent to the world.

Little Jimmy figured that if we could unload ten containers in one day, he would send ten drivers to the port. This seemed logical. If the terminal was having a bad day and each driver could get one container, he would be more likely to get all ten. However, this was not the logical, winning strategy it appeared to be.

However, we at the warehouse *assumed* that we could process ten inbound containers in a day. We thought that two drivers, each running a forklift, could handle them in roughly five hours. But we had been operating for less than a month. We were months away from having the experience to work that quickly.

To complicate matters more, after Little Jimmy's ten drivers went to the port together, they all came out of the port *together.* We only had four dock doors and the ramp, and not much yard space. When the trucks showed up, we filled up all four doors and had six trucks sitting in the street's turn lane on a busy arterial. The next four hours were a madhouse as we processed the drivers, got their trucks backed up to the dock doors, cut the container seals, unloaded cargo, handled documentation and signatures, etc.

"It's like wiping your bum with a hoop," Chester groaned. "There's no end to it!"

I handled the paperwork and directed truck traffic in the yard while Chester and Mutt unloaded the containers. Drivers began to get pissed because of the long delay. Tension was running high. When a driver with a heavy French accent came into the warehouse without a safety vest on, Chester made him get one from his cab. When the guy came back, he complained about Chester's tone. I thought Chester was going to throw punches at a guy forty years his junior. Instead, he barked at the driver to get back in his truck and wait for us to finish unloading his trailer.

"What was that about?" I asked Chester.

"I could tell he was from Quebec. I hate French-Canadians," Chester replied.

I knew that Chester was Canadian, but based on what I learned that day about his views of French-Canadians, I concluded that he was really a Canadian-Canadian.

We never saw that driver again, or any other driver from Quebec. We did have a lumber customer from Quebec. That person gave Chester a chance to go on occasional rants about French-Canadians. "*Bass-turds*" he'd say with a poorly imitated French accent. "Stupid frogs," he'd rant at other times. "They aren't *real* Canadians." It was hard to tell if Chester really had an issue with French-Canadians or if his rants were just a gag to entertain me at work. To this day, I don't know.

At the end of that tumultuous day, I realized that we had unloaded twelve containers, not ten. Apparently Little Jimmy had decided to send twelve drivers to the port, just to make sure he got at least ten containers. That made our day even tougher. The plan also backfired on him. He had to pay extra for the time that drivers waited at our warehouse.

Operations: Where all the plans that look good on paper go to die.

10

Security

All small business and startup owners who think about how to make money also want to prevent theft by unscrupulous employees or customers. Some businesses are more exposed to stealing, such as a restaurant or convenience store, and others might even be vulnerable to a flash mob bent on destroying a store and stealing everything that's not nailed down.

During our first year, the issue of security was low on our priority list. We were mostly focused on surviving. We gave our attention to operations, expanding our customer base, and establishing an identity. We refined our processes and planned for long-term growth.

Unfortunately, there were thieves.

Dirty, Rotten Scoundrels

Most people know how to be good. They don't cheat on their spouses, they don't steal, they don't lie (mostly), they don't kill people, and they wash their damn hands after they use the bathroom. But there are those who don't fall into the "most people" category. Some are conniving thieves.

Why is it so hard for some people to just say no to stealing? They seem to do mental flip-flops in order to justify bad behavior. They might think, *I stole it because I needed it more than the owner.* Or perhaps they think, *The person I stole it from is a bad person, so they deserve it.* Or maybe they just don't care about other people. That they rationalize such behavior is clearly a sign that they know they are doing the wrong thing, but they often stay on the immoral road.

Our initial security concerns were related to the types of products we housed. We worried about some products in our care, such as computers, but we didn't worry at all about Little Jimmy's supersacks full of resin. They had no value to a thief, and at 2500 pounds each, a thief would have almost no chance of getting one out of our warehouse.

Occasionally we'd lose things like bolt cutters. We'd loan one to a driver and never see it again. We started pasting our company logo on our stuff, which helped a bit. But someone intentionally stole our shop-vac. If anyone finds a yellow shop-vac with a Joel's Warehouse logo on it, please let me know. I still have the extra attachments stored in a box somewhere.

Someone also stole a fire extinguisher. To comply with the local fire code, we decided to upgrade our fire extinguishers and install them in easy-to-reach spots. We bought a half dozen of them. Chester put them near where he was mounting one on a wall. Then he took a bathroom break. Several minutes later he returned to find that an over-the-road driver had stolen one. He had already driven out of the parking lot before Chester noticed. What a jerk. I had thoughts of filling his cab with fire extinguisher foam.

Little Jimmy owned three trucks, which he parked at our warehouse. The lot was surrounded by a fence and had a locked gate. Early one morning, MP showed up to work and opened the gate. Shortly after that, someone brazenly walked in and stole one of Little Jimmy's trucks. When his driver arrived to work, he discovered his truck was gone.

A week later, someone reported an abandoned truck in a residential neighborhood fifteen miles from our warehouse. The police checked it out and called Little Jimmy to let him know they had found his vehicle. Apparently, the thief had been living in it for a few days. Condoms, clothing, and other crap littered the floor. The police dusted for prints and Little Jimmy's driver cleaned out the cab.

One of the objects in the cab was a vacuum, likely stolen, which we used in the office for years. Perhaps the universe was compensating us a little for our stolen shop-vac.

It Was an Accident

We sometimes lost money by damaging products. Accidents happen, which is a security issue. Accidents can be as costly to a company as theft. I'm not talking about deadly accidents, such as a supersack falling off a forklift and landing on a coworker. I'm talking about normal accidents.

Chester apparently had a grudge against warehouse door 1. To raise it the last two feet, it needed a strong nudge. We often left it open to help bring fresh air and light into the office, and so that we could see what was going on in the yard. If the person who opened it got lazy, it could spell trouble.

Chester got lazy one day and didn't nudge the door all the way up. While backing a raised forklift with a pallet out of a trailer, the forklift mast smashed into the door and seriously dented it. We were in the early weeks of our startup. The last thing we needed was to waste money on a $400 door repair. As the company owners, we paid for such repairs.

I told Chester to get a door repair company to fix it as soon as possible. Chester procrastinated, which turned out to be a good thing. Two weeks later, he did the same thing causing further damage. Eventually, the door repair company fixed the dent. They also improved the door's tension so that it would raise all the way without a nudge.

I soon discovered that these types of costly accidents occurred regularly, but we wouldn't find out about them from the culprit; we'd discover the damage ourselves. Sometimes people did not even know they had made the mistake, which made it hard to figure out a root cause.

So Chester and I assumed responsibility for every hole in the wall, broken rafter, busted door, or damaged freight.

As a result of the theft and accidents, we decided to invest in a security camera system.

The Camera Don't Lie

We bought an install-it-yourself camera system. Chester and I came in one weekend to run the cable and mount the cameras. The system had a digital recorder that we hooked up to a monitor and put in our electronics closet. I could also control the cameras remotely from any computer or a smartphone app.

I loved the system. That might say a thing or two about me, none of it good. I reviewed the recording every morning when I arrived at the warehouse. I especially looked for the motion detection checks in the middle of the night that would indicate there had been movement. Then I would click on that section of the recording and watch large specs of dust or moths flying by the camera.

Sometimes I would watch the previous days' activities at a higher speed. This way I could watch myself turning on the lights and, at the end of the day, turning off the lights. When I wasn't at the warehouse, I'd check the activity on my smartphone, just to see what was going on.

I often called Chester and told him I had seen something on the camera that I didn't like. Chester hated it. "You're on vacation!" he'd yell.

"I'm sitting at a bar having a beer. Don't worry about it."

"I'm hanging up now," Chester would say before the line went dead.

When I called fifteen minutes later, he usually would not answer the phone.

As a startup owner, I think my sickness was understandable,

because the stakes were so high. The business was my source of income. A serious mistake could put us into hot water. I trusted Chester, but the success of the business was everything. I couldn't stop thinking about it.

The camera system helped to eliminate some of my sleepless nights, but not all of them. I knew that a camera system could not stop people from stealing or making mistakes. It was just a tool to help prevent those things as much as possible. If something did happen, we would at least know what happened.

Even with the camera system, food theft in the breakroom continued. It was hard for me to believe, but in our small space with few employees, people would steal lunches. The employees knew about the security cameras, so they were never the culprits. However, over-the-road truck drivers would hit the bathroom and then swing through the breakroom to steal food and drinks out of the fridge while the forklift drivers were busy.

The odds of us ever seeing the same over-the-road truck driver twice were rare, which is perhaps why they stole so much food. Ironically, we had plenty of snacks and drinks available for the truckers, which we were happy to give away if they asked. I would give a person in need the shirt off my back if he asked, but when people steal from me, I lose all respect for them.

At times we stored loads of food and drink that had been rejected by local grocery stores. If a twelve pack of soda sprang a leak, the local store would reject the whole load and send it back to the grocery chain's distribution center. We were the fallback place for some manufacturers, reworking the load on their behalf by removing damaged or unsellable products so that the undamaged product could be redelivered.

Over the years we ended up with more soda than I can recall. We had tons of tortilla chips, salsa, ketchup, mustard, mayonnaise, candy, sunglasses, bleach, vinegar, flashlights, furniture, and . . . If a load was shipped or trucked in from thousands of miles away, it was often cheaper and easier to have the warehouse keep it than to send it back to its origin. (I miss this warehouse perk.)

We didn't always keep this stuff. Who needs six hundred bottles of ketchup? Instead, we donated it to local charities, foodbanks, or truck drivers. My kids' karate dojo ended up with a ton (a literal ton) of fruit juices that he gave to kids. There were plenty of people in need, so we gave most of it away.

The camera system also helped us expand our customer base. When customers with electronics products learned that we had cameras monitoring the warehouse 24/7, they became interested in working with us. The first electronics customer asked us to go a step further by adding a secure cage inside the warehouse. We rented one from a security fencing company for a year. Soon we housed gaming electronics worth millions of dollars, all under the watchful eye of a camera. Chester and I werc the only ones with keys to the lock on the cage.

The Camera Don't Lie: Part II

The cameras also provided us with accident documentation. In my experience, 99 percent of the accidents in our warehouse involved a forklift. They poked holes in sheetrock, damaged doors and freight, and damaged other forklifts.

Clang! The sound rang out as Chester and Mutt backed the Speedboat and the Tank into each other. One of them was trying to stage a pallet of supersacks for a loadout while the other was moving a pallet of soda out of storage for a donation pickup. Forklifts can't really hurt each other, but the two septuagenarians needed to pay better attention.

"No bullfighting!" I yelled at them from the office, using a line I learned from Mutt. He did not "operate" forklifts; rather, Mutt "mounted the bull." He didn't "drive" the forklift; rather, Mutt "rode the bull." At the end of a long day, Mutt was "tired of sitting on the bull." When he parked the forklift at the end of the day, he put "the bull in the barn."

The nice thing about "bulls" is that they are almost indestructible. Our large forklifts weighed close to ten-thousand pounds. The average small car (still much bigger than our forklifts) probably weighs 2500 pounds. Forklifts don't do anything fast, but they apply a lot of force to get the work done. When a forklift bumped into a door rail, we had a rail to fix. With a simple mistake while driving around a parking lot, a forklift could easily put a hole into the side of a car. I love forklifts, but we had to respect them.

When these types of accidents occurred, almost no

one confessed. Video gave us the answers that we could use to help prevent more accidents. We could address a reckless forklift driver. We could hold a conversation about forklift safety. We could see if our stacking arrangements could be improved.

I must acknowledge the safety success of our warehouse. We had zero injuries for as long as we ran the company—if you exclude Little Jimmy showing us how to do bulk loadouts. In an industrial environment, that is hard to do. I'm glad that I never had to review an injury.

I once reviewed the video recordings to see what Chester's new girlfriend looked like. He had previously denied that she existed, but I caught him on camera, late in the evening, showing off the warehouse and forklifts to his woman. Thankfully, that's all I caught them doing.

Middle of the Night

As the startup owner, I was on the hook for anything that happened, regardless of the hour. Sometimes the security system would set off an alarm and I would have to attend to the situation in the middle of the night.

My cell phone would ring. Squinting at the clock on the nightstand, I would realize it was 12:35 a.m. The security monitoring company would verify my identity, inform me about the alarm, and ask if I wanted them to call the police. I would tell them to turn off the alarm and that I would go check things out.

This occurred every couple of weeks for years. Each time, I dutifully got dressed and went down to the warehouse to check it out, only to find out there was nothing going on. The culprit? Sometimes a strong gust of wind would trip the security contacts on a dock door. One door in particular, door 17, held a special place in a dark area of my soul. I hated that door. It messed with my life for months.

There was also the fire alarm. The law required us to have two forms of communication between the alarm company and the fire alarm. We used a standard phone line and a VOIP line. For some reason, the VOIP line would reset in the middle of the night every couple of weeks. It was probably a software update. When the line lost connection, it would trigger a warning at the fire alarm company. The fire alarm company would call the landlord. The landlord would call me. I would go down to the warehouse to ensure that there were no problems. After four months of this, the landlord told the alarm company to stop contacting him. I ended up going down to the warehouse a half dozen times in the middle of the night.

There were also times when someone left the gate or a warehouse door open—all night. Usually, we'd get a call from a neighbor or else Chester would catch it on his drive back home from the club. Fortunately, the commute from his evening hangout spot to his home took him right past the warehouse.

11

Accounts Receivable

Accounts receivable, despite the boring wording, was my favorite part of owning a business. I loved to bill customers. I loved to crunch numbers and add up revenue. Like the good little capitalist that I am, I enjoyed seeing the business growing and turning a profit every year. I also loved investing revenue back into the company and then watching the accounts receivable numbers grow even larger.

Accounts receivable (AR) is where dreams happen. By contrast, accounts payable is where dreams go to die. It's hard to discuss one without the other, but I'm going to focus on AR first.

Living the AR Dream

As I said earlier, I am frustrated when people say they are living the dream while they are slaving away at a thankless job. Living the dream must involve more than being "warm, dry, and employed," as one person often told me. Let's be real. It is easier to live your dreams when you have money. And that means that you should focus on AR.

The first principle of AR, as I learned in my other jobs, is to bill your customers as soon as possible. One company I used to work for had two major shipping days each week: Wednesday and Friday. On those days, people in the billing department would start at 8 a.m. and work until 10 p.m. so that they could immediately send out the bills for each week's shipments. The sooner that invoices were sent to customers, the sooner the clock would start ticking on their thirty-day payment deadlines. Sometimes getting paid quickly is a matter of survival.

As a small business owner, I found it important to keep two sets of books. I am not implying that you operate like the mob, with one set of books for paying taxes and a second book for off-the-record transactions related to cocaine and hookers. Like any self-respecting and upstanding business owner, I expensed drugs and prostitutes through the company, which lowered our profits and thus our tax liability. (Smile.)

When I suggest using a second set of books, I'm referring to an official accounting system. I recorded the numbers on an accrual basis, meaning that I recorded revenue on the day I billed the customer, and I recorded the expenses on the day that I received an invoice from a vendor.

Then, on a spreadsheet, I duplicated the dollar amounts on a cash basis by projecting how much money I expected to receive during a given week. Later I would record what was paid that week. For accounts payable, I recorded what I expected to pay each week based on the due date of the vendor's invoice. In other words, I recorded what happened on the day it happened. Then I could see the whole picture of everything that had been recorded to that point. On the spreadsheet, I tried to *project* what was going to happen weeks and months ahead. Then I recorded what really happened.

In the next chapter, I will discuss accounts payable in more detail, but recording all the numbers twice allowed me to see whether I would have the money in the bank to cover the expenses. To "live the dream," I needed to have money left after I had caught up on AP.

There are several strategies for maximizing AR, but one of the most important is to get paid for the work that has been billed. It does not work to do $50,000 of work in one month if someone can't pay $10,000 of those bills. How did we manage that?

Managing Credit Risk

Over the years, we did millions of dollars in business and ended up writing off less than $5,000 of it in bad debt. Anyone in collections would be proud of that number. It was one part skill, and two parts luck. We only had one total bust, and we did not feel that bad about it.

A transactional business, like a restaurant or grocery store, involves much less risk when it comes to getting paid. Customers use cash or credit cards to pay when the product or service is delivered. There is more risk of not getting paid in business-to-business environments.

Our main protection against credit failures was that people generally wanted, and needed, a long-term relationship with us. We also wanted long-term relationships with our vendors. So, when someone was slow to pay, we tried to work with them over the course of months to make sure we got every dollar.

We also had a legal advantage. If a customer didn't pay us, and if we still had his product in our warehouse, we could claim it for ourselves until he paid. However, that rarely occurred because most freight was moved in and out of the warehouse within days—weeks before payment was due. We did our due diligence early because our leverage decreased after the freight left.

Large companies use professional resources to verify credit worthiness. That was not us. We relied on instinct and common sense to determine whether someone was a credit risk. Many of our customers probably didn't have a record with the reporting agencies anyway. We had to extend a lot of trust. Thankfully, our clients rarely abused that trust.

Our major failure involved a character named Doc. He was one of those transoceanic guys who was born in Europe, went to college in the Americas, and regularly flew back and forth between the US and Europe. He was highly educated, spoke several languages, had many ideas and lots of energy, and was possibly full of shit.

The Doc

Doc told us he owned a farm in Europe where he cultivated horseradish. He wanted to import horseradish root in refrigerated containers and have us transload it into domestic reefer trucks. The root would be delivered to local manufacturers who would turn it into a more consumable form. He also said that his farm processed bulk horseradish powder. His idea was to import fifty-pound bags of the powder and sell them to manufacturers who would convert it into consumer-friendly bottles.

Neither Chester nor I knew much about horseradish, but we did have commonsense questions. We wanted to know how it could be profitable to import horseradish from overseas as opposed to just growing it in the US?

Doc had an explanation. He said his wife's uncle administered the tariffs in his home country. He would be able to export the horseradish without paying taxes. He added that his home country in Europe had abundant cheap labor and no pesky labor laws or minimum wages.

Doc accepted the fact that our facility was not refrigerated. To compensate, he agreed to work with us to ensure that the inbound container and outbound trailer (both refrigerated) arrived at the warehouse simultaneously. He said there were two forty-foot containers of horseradish root on the water already. We scheduled to transload the product a week later.

Chester pointed out that we would probably have a hard time fitting two forty-foot-containers of product into one fifty-three-foot trailer. Thus, it would cost more if we had to break down pallets and hand stack the freight. Doc said he that he was willing to come with his teenage son and do the labor himself. Apparently, Doc had a nearby apartment where he stayed when he wasn't traveling.

Chester and I took a real liking to Doc. He seemed to be an earnest and honest guy. His story had some holes in it, but he was passionately trying to get a business off the ground, which we could understand. We decided to trust him. Our financial exposure was relatively low—just labor and warehouse space. If he was a flash in the pan, we wouldn't be out any hard dollars.

On the day of the transload, two containers showed up with horseradish roots and the outbound trucker showed up with the reefer trailer. Doc also showed up with his teenage son to help lump boxes. As Chester predicted, there was not enough room in the reefer for all the product. We ended up with eight pallets of horseradish left over. Little did we know that it would haunt us for years.

Doc disappeared for a couple of weeks. When he returned, he said that he had dried horseradish on the way. He had been back to the farm in Europe to make sure that the harvest was going well. He showed us the pictures on his phone.

We received twenty pallets of powdered horseradish at about the time when Doc's first bill was due. There were about twenty boxes on each pallet, and each pallet had one fifty-pound bag of horseradish powder in it. Doc grabbed a couple of boxes to take to his customers as samples. He apologized for not paying his bill for the horseradish root and promised he would take care of it.

Doc shared more stories about his farm in Europe and said that he would like to fly us out there to show us around. He had big plans to ship hundreds of containers per year through our warehouse, distributing horseradish all over the

United States. Chester was sold on taking the trip to Europe, especially when Doc mentioned they could hit the casinos and completely debauch themselves. I volunteered to stay behind and run the warehouse.

So began a regular pattern with Doc. He would talk about upcoming contracts, plans to move his freight, and promises to pay us as soon as he had the money. He had plenty of excuses, usually involving the failure of his customers to pay him. Other excuses included wire transfers that were blocked by the government, bank mistakes, and money going to the wrong place. He continued to show us pictures of his visits to the farm while talking about his plans to import other crops from his farm, which would certainly make us all rich. Chester and I knew it was all talk, but it was entertaining.

Chester continued to tease Doc about the trip to Europe and Doc kept making promises. Months passed. His storage bill got larger. Doc visited less and less. We would leave voicemail messages. Then he would show up with more stories and promises. It became clear to us that he didn't have an executable business plan. He couldn't find anyone who wanted the horseradish root at his prices.

Whenever Doc came in, I passed him off to Chester so that they could bullshit about the trip they would never take to Europe. Chester got tired of that and started passing him off to Mutt. Doc and Mutt would talk about selling horseradish to grocery chains. Mutt tried to volley Doc back to Chester or me.

Remember those eight pallets of horseradish root? They were slowly disintegrating. The pallets were shrink wrapped.

We could see the condensation building up on the inside of the wrap. Rotting horseradish liquid seeped through the boxes, causing them to warp. Finally, the eight pallets of horseradish root had to be dumped. I had no idea what it looked like inside the boxes, and I didn't want to know.

We continued to press Doc for payment. As usual we left a voicemail. A few days later he showed up full of stories about a new scheme that involved a casino at a mountain resort that was accessible only by helicopter. He already had partners with money. They would rely on his supposed government connections to get a gaming license. He would keep 25 percent of the profit and make tens of millions per year. He and Chester would fly there as soon as it opened and have an exciting time.

Finally, we told him we were done holding his freight. He needed to get his product out of the warehouse, or we would dump it. Doc promised to return with a plan within two weeks, but we never saw or heard from him again.

Doc was not the only self-proclaimed emperor with no clothes we encountered, but he was the only one to bamboozle us. Luckily, our loss only involved some space in the warehouse and our time.

The Entrepreneur

Then there was the entrepreneur who had a plan to buy military surplus computer equipment (up to fifteen years old). He aimed to sell this equipment to South American countries where the expired military equipment would be better than the old tech used in some of those nations.

This guy wanted to hire us to transload the equipment for export. Therefore, we would not have any leverage (i.e., his freight) if he didn't pay his bill. We decided that we would have to be paid up front. The entrepreneur agreed to those terms, and he understood that he might need to pay additional charges for driver standby time.

I figured that he would not pay for driver standby time, so I compensated by quoting a high price for the transload work. I also sensed that we would do a bunch of freight rehandling, so I increased the quoted price even more. He agreed to the cost and said he would transfer the money to us.

I ended up being right on both counts. The freight showed up loosely palletized. After we emptied the fifty-three-foot trailer, we were forced to restack every computer and monitor and shrink-wrap it. Only then would it fit into a container and not bounce around on the ocean voyage.

When the container was delivered to the port, the driver had two hours of standby time. I tried to recoup $130 from the entrepreneur. He never responded to emails or phone calls. We never saw him again.

Liquored Up

As you should be learning by now, credit risk often depends on the character of your clients. We once worked with four characters who were selling bottled liquor out of the overseas shipping market, in which Chester and I had spent years working. I'll call them the Bottler, the Distributor, the Shipper, and the Money Guy.

The role of the Bottler was to handle physical operations at the bottling plant overseas. The Shipper was responsible for getting the product to the US via an international shipping line. The Distributor was responsible for distributing the liquor in the US. The Money Guy, a native of an Asian country (important later), was responsible for raising the capital to make all this work.

I never met the Bottler, but Chester flew to the overseas location to meet him, Chester wanted to verify the operation's existence and to check references. The deal was too big and seemed too unrealistic for us to rely on gut instinct. They expected to ship dozens of containers per week, which would be stored and transloaded in our warehouse for nationwide distribution. We did not want to get stuck with dozens of containers of booze in our warehouse and no payment.

The Bottler was a character. Chester took an immediate liking to him. He had a plaque on his desk with a Winston Churchill quote: "All I can say is that I have taken more out of alcohol than alcohol has taken out of me." Our confidence in him grew as we learned that he was shipping out many pallets of liquor while also handling the bottling operations for several other customers. He was a solid, long-term operator.

We confirmed that the Shipper had an arrangement with the international shipping line and that his containers were hitting the water. Chester verified this through his connections at the shipping line, which had extended credit to the Shipper. They had some concerns, however, and we soon found out why.

At first, we weren't sure the Distributor was committed to using our services. He was the only one of the four who lived near us, and he had considered doing the warehousing himself. Then we realized the actual bad news: The group needed financing. None of the four seemed to have much money and they did not have any committed customers yet, a big red flag. We were surprised that the Bottler didn't finance the operation, but we figured that perhaps he had kicked in 25 percent and expected the others to pony up their shares as well.

In an amazing twist of events, Doc (remember him?) happened to be at the warehouse when the Distributor, the Shipper, and the Money Guy came by to visit. The Money Guy was talking about expanding his plans. In addition to distributing liquor, he also wanted to distribute sugar, wheat, and other things by using his connections in Asia. Doc got interested in the conversation. He and the Money Guy talked for a while, trying to see if there was some synergy in their business ideas.

Doc approached us later and said he wouldn't do business with these guys because they had no idea what they were doing. They were "full of shit," he said. Doc was right. Perhaps it took one to know one.

The first containers of booze started arriving at the port, but the shipping line would not release them until they were paid for the ocean transit. Depending on who we talked to, we were told that that the freight was coming to us next, or that the Distributor was going to take it and our services would not be needed. In either situation, it seemed unlikely that the containers would leave the port soon.

In a subsequent visit to the Bottler, Chester realized that he was extending credit to the other three and selling product to them at the wholesale price. He had bottled the liquor, loaded the containers, and taken them to the port, but he had not been paid for any of that. Unsurprisingly, he was done working for the other three until they paid their bills.

A few weeks passed and we heard that the Money Guy was meeting with a bunch of investors to bring the whole thing back on track—paying the ocean line and the Bottler— and then use our services. At that point, we decided to require payment in advance, to make sure that we did not get stuck with the liquor and no payment. The ocean line still had dozens of containers at the port. The booze had been sitting there for weeks.

After we received the update about the group's financial plan to raise capital, we did not hear anything again for weeks. Chester paid another visit to the Bottler and finally got the rest of the story. The Money Guy had successfully raised $400,000 in capital from some investors in California. For a few days it looked like the venture would survive, and that the vendors would get paid. The money was in the bank for a day or two, at which point the Money Guy emptied the bank account. He then absconded with all the money to his home in Asia, where no one could contact him. Legal recourses were few due to rocky relations between his home country and the US. As far as I, know neither the Bottler nor the steamship line was ever paid a dime. I don't know what happened to the containers of liquor.

In conclusion, I encourage you to carefully manage your accounts receivable. That aspect of business can either make your dreams come true or be your worst nightmare. We were lucky that we had so few hiccups along the way.

12

Accounts Payable

Accounts payable is not nearly as fun as accounts receivable. All you do with AP is watch money go out the door. But there is truth in the old saying that you need to "spend money to make money." Thus, AP is a necessary evil. It is just as important as AR. Relationships with vendors are important, and those relationships do not mean squat if you don't pay them.

When running a startup, it is common to have trouble paying the bills on time. We had some strategies for dealing with that.

Timing

The first hurdle to paying bills is, obviously, to have sufficient money in the bank to cover the payments. Even when a company is making moncy, it can be difficult to pay vendors on time.

I learned this lesson at a prior job. The more money we made, the bigger our problems became. We increasingly faced timing issues between paying vendors and receiving money from customers. We gave our customers thirty days from the date of billing to pay us, and our vendors gave us the same terms. In theory, everything should work out within a few days of each other. A healthy business should be able to bankroll enough cash to make that gap a nonissue.

I said *should*. At my previous employer, we faced a problem caused by our biggest customer, which at one point generated approximately 10 percent of company's revenue. By the time I left to start Joel's Warehouse, that number had increased to 50 percent of the revenue. The customer was a Fortune 100 company that insisted on paying vendors in forty-five to sixty days. If we wanted to do business with this company, we had to comply with their non-negotiable terms. Thus, ironically, our rapid growth made it harder to pay our bills.

Because this important customer (50 percent of the business) only paid us every fifty days or so, we struggled to catch up with our vendor payments that were due every thirty days. After the first month of rapid growth, we were in the hole by $300,000. By the fourth month, the hole grew to $875,000.

By the fifth month, our Fortune 100 customer would pay us for approximately two months' worth of invoices, enabling us to catch up on the AP and leaving us with $150,000. Everything should have been fine, right? Nope. We would not expect payments for the next month's growth. By month six, we were $725,000 behind on vendor payments again. At the end of one year, we had made $3.8 million on $31.8 million in sales, but we were $1.2 million in the hole with our vendors because we had no cash. The Fortune 100 customer owed us millions that they would eventually pay, but we could not pay our bills. It was ridiculous.

The vendors we needed the most hated how bad we were at keeping up with payments. I tried to explain the problem, but they didn't quite understand, or they didn't see it as their problem. Perhaps they were scared that we were losing money and might default on what we owed. We knew that we *could* pay them, but we never knew *when.*

Ultimately, my boss decided to work with a factoring company that would pay us within twenty days for what the Fortune 100 customer owed us. In exchange for a percentage of the revenue, the factoring company would accept payment from the Fortune 100 customer in fifty days. The factoring company's percentage hurt our overall profits, but we did not have a choice. We had to stay in the good graces of our vendors.

I suggested to my boss that we start putting aside a cash reserve of our own. This would allow us to act as our own factoring company and avoid losing several percentage points of profit. I have no idea whether this idea was implemented because I left shortly thereafter to start Joel's Warehouse.

Before that experience with my previous employer, it had never occurred to me that success could be painful. I resolved at Joel's Warehouse to not fall into the same trap. That was easier said than done. It was also the reason I kept two sets of books, one for the accrued earnings and the second to track cash flow.

Lesson Learned

I like another old saying, even if it is not always practical: "Neither a lender nor a borrower be." Again, though not always practical, I tried to treat our startup according to that phrase.

For example, as we launched our startup, we leased forklifts instead of buying them and making payments. I don't normally like the idea of leasing, but I also don't like paying interest. We leased the Speedboat for all the years we were in business. Perhaps we could have saved money if we had bought that forklift outright, as we did with the Tank and several iterations of the Beast. We leased other forklifts, like the Green Machine, the squeeze clamp, and the Terry for varying periods to cover immediate needs.

In general, we leased until we could afford to buy with cash. No interest payments. No five-year terms. Forklifts don't depreciate quickly, so when we sold the company, we basically recovered what we paid for them. The same applied to many other items we purchased, such as the dock plates, pallet jacks, container jack, and yard hostler.

By buying forklifts, we could keep our monthly AP number lower, which reduced our risk of being unable to pay all the bills. I wanted most of our costs to be variable as opposed to fixed; that is, the costs would be generated in synch with the revenue stream. For example, I would pay for port trucking as our client paid for our services.

Our first real test, however, came with a period of rapid growth, after our first year of business. We acquired the lumber business and tripled in size overnight. How did we end up eating a fish twice our size? It is a long story, but from a financial perspective, we arranged to buy the assets up front with cash (no loans or other fixed recurring payments). We then agreed to a multiyear deal by which we paid a spiff for every lumber load we exported (a variable expense).

I immediately set out to change the operation by adding a new trucking vendor into the mix. The trucking vendor put us on fifteen-day payment terms. Within twenty-five days, we owed him $100,000 and we were ten days past due on the first invoices. The obvious reason was because our customers had terms to pay us after thirty days, and I hadn't been paid for any of our work yet. The owner of the trucking company came to see me.

With my two sets of books at hand, I knew that in a week I would receive enough payment from customers to pay all the trucking invoices. By being fiscally conservative for the next few weeks, I knew I could build up a cash reserve that would allow me to float through our expected growth.

When the owner of the trucking company sat down at my desk, I turned my computer monitor around and showed him the spreadsheet. I explained that my customers paid me at thirty days and that I would in turn, pay him at thirty days. He could see my honesty and agreed to give me thirty days to pay. We never had an issue again. In fact, he came back a few weeks later with a bunch of smoked salmon and thanked me for my business. The guys in the warehouse devoured it in an hour.

As we continued to grow, Joel's Warehouse never fell into that hole again. I always kept our reservoir of cash full, and

I kept our terms for customers and vendors even so that we could stay on top of the AP.

In the third year, our system was tested again. We picked up XYZ mattress company. We did thirty loads per week, lots of storage, port trucking, lumper labor, palletizing, shrink-wrapping, and custom labelling for them. They had just established their first office in the United States, so they had no idea how they were going to pay their bills.

We spent a ton of money serving this customer, which represented 25 percent of our volume. Soon they had surpassed Little Jimmy as our number one customer by revenue, if not in our hearts. But after sixty days, we had not received a single check from them. They communicated with me daily. Soon we had hundreds of pallets of their product stored in our warehouse, with hundreds more inbound over the next weeks.

I kept up the steady pressure to get paid, but I tried not to be overbearing. They asked for patience. After about seventy days they sent a check that covered the first thirty days of invoices. It was the largest single check we had ever received. A week later, another check arrived that completely paid what they owned us. We never had another problem with them.

I was extremely happy that our reservoir of cash had held us up. However, that was the price of growth. I'd seen it before. I had learned that cash is leverage.

Leverage

For obvious reasons, AP is linked tightly to vendor relationships. Your ability to pay your vendor on time, with a minimum of fuss, creates an opening for savings in other ways. You can leverage your status as a good customer to get support you otherwise might not find.

For example, our primary forklift vendor sold us the Beast II for $30,000. He came by to deliver the invoice. Then he casually observed, "There's some guy standing in your parking lot in his underwear, hitting golf balls across the street."

"What?!" I exclaimed, while choking on my coffee. I rushed over to the window and observed Mutt chipping golf balls over the road and into the wooded park—wearing nothing but his underwear. I opened the window and yelled at him. "What are you doing!?"

"Getting rid of a couple of extra balls," Mutt replied. He tossed his golf club back into his trunk, grabbed a change of clothes off the front dash of his car, and dressed himself for playing handball at the club.

"Jesus, Mary, and Joseph," I blasphemed. I turned to the forklift vendor and shook my head.

The vendor laughed and handed me the invoice. "I just want to know how you're going to take care of this," he said.

"I'll call up your front desk gal and give her the company credit card number," I said. I paid our monthly lease on the Speedboat this way. The credit card would get a 1 percent cash back reward for the $30,000 Beast II purchase.

"Uh, well, uh . . . I don't want to pay the card fees," our

vendor stammered. "How about we do half on the credit card and the other half by check?"

Now I had a dilemma. I liked using the cash back reward for buying pizzas and other staff treats, but it was important to preserve a good relationship with our vendor. I knew he would probably pay 3 percent in card fees. The key to this negotiation was to understand what he could do for me in exchange.

"How about you give us the first four preventative maintenance services for free and I will write you a check for the whole thing right now?" I said.

The forklift vendor looked at Chester, who had wandered into to the office after hearing me yell at Mutt, and praised my negotiating skills. "You see this guy?" he asked Chester. "This is how you negotiate. Joel, you have a deal."

I wrote him a check for the $30,000 and everyone was happy. The real value at play was hidden—the value of vendor relations. The vendor's credit card fees would have been about $900. I knew that the four maintenance services would cost a $1000 in total. That was a good trade for losing the $300 in cash back rewards. There was benefit for him too. He was willing to offer the four free maintenance services because his incremental cost was much lower than the credit card fees. Moreover, he would not need to explain to his boss why he accepted a $900 credit card fee. It proved to be a win-win. The art of negotiation is understanding the position of the person on the other side of the table.

It is also important to make sure that AP is in order when building relationships with new vendors. Many will ask for credit references, banking info, and other relevant items to prove your creditworthiness. I was always ready to provide that information when needed. It might sound stupid, but I asked my reference vendors for permission to use them as a reference.

A new vendor would usually ask our old vendor whether we paid on time. If our current vendors trusted us, which they did, then we had leverage.

Many small companies struggle to pay. They have no leverage at all. As J. Paul Getty once said, "If you owe the bank $100, that's your problem. If you owe the bank $100 million, that's the bank's problem." Banks (or other vendors) will typically do what is needed to never allow customers to owe them enough to become their problem. Unpaid vendors will cut off clients before they become a big issue. Then the indebted company will gain a bad reputation and find it impossible to win new business. At that point, the business might collapse.

On the flip-side, I worked for a large company whose second largest customer was always in arrears, owing millions on sixty-day payment terms. My employer worked with this delinquent payor for years. Finally, my company gave up. We bought the customer for an undisclosed amount, perhaps more than $100 million. I guarantee that all the vendors were thrilled when a company with money took it over.

Profit

I feel the need to defend the word *profit*. It often gets a bad rap. That's because some people do unethical things to get it. But profit earned honestly is good. Most of the vendors we worked with, including the forklift vendor described in this chapter, were honestly running their businesses.

It is important to remember that profits can rise and fall from year to year. Startup owners often keep only a fraction of a certain year's profit so that they can reinvest in the company. It's important for us to remember that profit is usually money that supports jobs—at the startup and at the vendors. Profits, in short, support families and communities.

Finally, it is important to consider that startup owners assume major risks. Profit is the reward for that risk, as it should be. If Joel's Warehouse could not turn a profit, Chester and I could have lost our homes.

I still wonder how anyone could have the bravery to start a business.

13

Government Relations

We have all heard that only death and taxes are certain, but your business relationship with the government is going to run deeper than just taxes. In my experience, there could be a hundred ways for the government to be involved in a startup.

If you're a sole proprietor without employees, you might only need to worry about the taxes. However, if your business has a location and employees, you should be prepared for a barrage of rules and regulations, inspection visits, and taxes that you never knew about. The government will hit you from all sides. The only thing you can do is survive.

Rules, Regulations, Permits

Warehouses are governed by the Uniform Commercial Code, Article 7. This code pertains to bills of lading, product ownership, liens against the product for non-payment, and so forth. Basically, our bill of lading (BOL) template had to include certain terms and information, otherwise the government would not be happy, and we would be more susceptible to lawsuits.

To become a bonded warehouse, and to do customs work for the US government, we were required to follow the Code of Federal Regulations, Title 19. If we wanted to own our trucks, we needed to comply with the CFR's Title 49.

We also needed to follow OSHA rules, which often involved minutia. For example, we were allowed to leave the dock doors open to get fresh air without adding a safety railing system because a person at our dock would fall less than four feet. We had to measure. Thankfully, our dock doors were a few inches less than four feet off the ground.

Startup owners need to understand the OSHA obligations that pertain to each type of business. Depending on the size of the company, the owner could be required to file incident reports, hold regular safety meetings, and pay for worker's compensation. Complying with requirements for some industries can be very time consuming.

When I worked at a different warehousing company, I invited the OSHA inspector to verify our compliance. Under OSHA's rules, any violations found during a site visit that was initiated by the company could not result in a fine. The inspector would note any deficiencies and give the company a time frame for correction. In general, OSHA's job is to protect people from getting hurt, so they would rather work with companies than fine them.

However, if a company catches OSHA's attention because of an accident, or if an OSHA inspection finds a bunch of violations, the company can expect to be on the long-term OSHA watch list. That happened to my buddy who ran a heavy-lift operation. Once the local OSHA inspector hit him with a couple of fines, my friend endured inspection visits every six months. In his words, it was like "getting nitpicked."

This OSHA approach is understandable. They admit to being understaffed. They do not have time to search every company for violations. So they focus on tracking the companies with known problems.

The city fire department had its own rules for governing our warehouse. These rules related to the commodities we stored and to the capability of our fire suppression system. The warehouse we occupied had been used to store fireworks fifteen years earlier, so our fire suppression system was excellent. Unfortunately, the fire department still showed up every quarter to ask us if we were storing fireworks, in addition to their normal annual inspections. We could not remove our location from their list of potential warehouses with fireworks.

Regarding inspections, the government can pass a law requiring annual fire inspections and then bill the company $500 for each one. Let me repeat: They can mandate inspections and then force companies to pay the bill. Apparently, all the other taxes don't cover that activity.

In addition, the law requires a commercial company to have its fire system inspected and repaired, if needed, annually. Otherwise, we could lose our permit with the city. We needed a professional monitoring service, with two separate lines of communication connected to that company.

We also had to have a permit, issued by the state's environmental department, for the property's stormwater drains. We had to pay the state an extra amount because seagulls pooped on our roof. When it rained, gull poop mixed with the rain. The rain ran down the gutter, flowed across our parking lot, into the storm drain, and out to sea. When we first took over the warehouse, our annual permit fee was more than $2000 per year, which seemed excessive. Our predecessors informed us that we might be required to take samples of drain water and send them to the state environmental agency.

We think the previous tenants of our warehouse had fallen afoul of a state environmental inspector. Once they had landed on the inspector's list, they had to follow onerous water testing requirements and pay heftier fees for stormwater drain use. Every six months, the inspector would harangue them if he saw any drops of oil on the pavement. As a warehouse, they had dozens of trucks per day drive through their yard. It was beyond their control to prevent trucks from dropping oil on their lot.

All this environmental activity stopped after we took over the warehouse. We called the state agency and, because we were a small business, got them to reduce our yearly permit to about $300. We regularly paid for our permit and tried to avoid giving them reasons to send an inspector. They also said that we did not need to test storm drain water. (I've always found it safer, from a legal perspective, to place dead bodies directly into the river and let them float out to international waters.)

Many government regulations affect the transportation of freight. For example, overseas shippers need to use the maximum amount of container space to keep costs low. So, it is not unusual for freight within a container to weigh more than is legally allowed for road transport, particularly if the load is "reducible." A single piece of machinery that weighs sixty thousand pounds surpasses the forty-three-thousand pound over-the-road weight limit, but it can't be taken apart (reduced) to comply with the weight limits. However, a container of supersacks weighing fifty thousand pounds can be reduced by removing some of the supersacks.

This is often how our warehouse helped overseas shippers. Loads from overseas would weigh too much for road transport, so we would transload the freight into over-the-road trucks so the freight could head to its destination. However, these overweight loads were technically illegal on the route between the port and the warehouse. Therefore, local governments designated the port area a "heavy haul corridor." By buying a permit from the local port authority, truckers could legally pull the loads between the shipping terminal and a nearby warehouse to be "reduced" for further transport.

When we took over the lumber business, we also gained a new government friend from the Department of Agriculture. Before any lumber could be shipped overseas, the government inspector had to make sure the wood was bug free. The shippers had to pay for each inspection. This was not a "service" otherwise covered by taxes, but it was legally required.

Then there were the business and incorporation licenses. The state needed its yearly fee for the corporation and the city needed its yearly business licensing fee. We also had a business license for another state where we thought we might work but never did. At least that state didn't ask us for weekly reporting, or I would have worn out the zero on my keyboard.

A trucking company that leased office space from us hung up their business sign on our fence. A few weeks later, the city notified them that they needed to register their business. They had recently moved from a neighboring city where they already had a business license. I still wonder how the city could react so quickly to the arrival of a new business. This was not a small town. Whatever the case, they were quick to collect business license fees and quarterly tax revenue.

We also had to pay an annual fee to a private company to maintain our SCAC code, which was our federal government registration as a freight forwarder. On top of that, we had to pay a yearly fee directly to the government to be registered as a freight forwarder. And every year we had to renew an insurance bond to be a freight forwarder. To sum up the tally, we had to pay two private entities before we could have the privilege of paying the federal government so that we could move freight.

As you can see, there are many government layers. They each have their rules and regulations and permits and fees. If startup owners don't purchase the permits, then they will be breaking a law—laws that were created for the purpose of selling permits.

After all that, you get to pay taxes.

Taxes

The city also wanted their part of our business. They taxed our "worldwide gross income." Perhaps for this reason there weren't many large companies located in the city. Why should a company be taxed for revenue generated in another part of the world?

The county also wanted their property taxes. We paid property taxes via our warehouse rent on the real property, and we had to pay property taxes to the county for items used to conduct business, such as personal property. We had to keep an inventory of computers, pencils, and whatever else we used to conduct business and then paid the county for the privilege of having it all. In the county where we operated, we could never truly own anything. We could purchase supplies and equipment, but then we had to pay the government for the right to use it. I find it shocking that people in government think that scheme is okay. As a business "owner," I carried all the risks but never owned anything.

At the state level, the government wanted their "use" taxes, and their business and occupation (B&O) taxes. The use tax was applied to purchases of products or services if sales tax was not paid at the time of purchase. We would pay the tax if we used the product rather than reselling it. To save money, some business owners would get a state reseller's permit and present that to any vendor from whom they purchased products. They never intended to resell the products, but it helped them avoid the 10 percent sales tax.

The state got wise and started making it harder to get a

reseller's permit. We had a reseller's permit that we used only for buying shipping containers that we intended to sell in another state where we held a business license. None of our plans worked out. Eventually our state would not renew the permit—because we were not using it.

Then the B&O tax was also tacked on every year in lieu of a state income tax on businesses. This "occupation" tax required us to pay a percentage of our gross income every quarter to the state.

In addition, we paid state unemployment taxes and worker's compensation. At the end of each quarter, we had to report how much we had just paid them in that same quarter. Why? Did they not keep track of what we had just paid? We wondered why they couldn't do the math without our help.

Did I mention federal payroll taxes? We paid a payroll company to handle these payments, along with our state-level worker's compensation. At the end of the year, we had our accountant look over our books and certify the personal income that would pass through to Chester and me. We were an S Corporation, so all the earnings were divided between us and charged at our personal tax rates.

A small trucking company or an independent contractor with one truck could experience government regulation misery. The ports around the country implemented clean air initiatives that forced older trucks to be taken out of commission or undergo expensive engine conversions. We all want clean air, but these regulations could completely decimate trucking firms.

The original government rule stated that truck engines

older than 1994 had to be decommissioned or converted. Then the government set the bar to 2012. Thus, an independent contractor with a truck built in 2010, which had just been paid off after a seven-year loan, would be screwed. The dream of using the truck to make money without paying a $1500 monthly payment would be crushed by the government requirement.

Port authorities delayed the new standard a couple of times because they knew it would force too many businesses and small contractors to quit, leaving a massive driver shortage in its wake. However, larger companies, which had already invested in newer trucks, pressured port officials to implement the new rule. They clearly hoped to eliminate their smaller competitors. This is a predictable and common result of government rulemaking; it crushes small business and enriches large businesses. Never has this been more apparent than during Covid-19 lockdowns. Many large businesses and retailers remained open whereas small businesses were shut down. Many were never able to reopen.

With so many government fees and rules to consider, I set up a spreadsheet showing the government entity, the tax, permit type, report type, and due dates for it all. Otherwise, I would have lost track of all the obligations. I, along with help from my accountant, did my honest best to comply with everything correctly. So far, no governments have contacted me about problems. I am keeping my fingers crossed until the statute of limitations expires.

Some folks argue that these taxes are good, that the government provides lots of services in exchange for the tax money. Blah, blah, blah. Yes, I like roads and police and fire protection. But this is a humorous book about my startup company trying to survive. This is not a civics class. So, let me tell you about the great government services we got at the warehouse.

Government Services

Besides the firefighters who kept asking about the fireworks we never had, or the inspectors who billed us to look through our warehouse, we didn't have much official contact with emergency services. We didn't have any medical emergencies or need for the police. Given our location on a main road near the port, there were constant patrols through the area. Our location seemed safe.

On one side of our warehouse property, a rail spur crossed the road near our lot and ran near our fence to serve a lumber company and a recycling company. Every day a train delivered empty rail cars and took away loaded rail cars. There were no rail crossing signs, or guard arms to block traffic, or warning lights to indicate that a train was coming.

Sometimes the railroad would deploy a worker to block traffic before the train went through, but usually the train blasted its horn and rolled slowly across the road. This made it difficult to hold phone conversations and caused temporary tinnitus.

The occasional idiot driver would accelerate to beat the train, but I never witnessed or heard about an accident. The train usually only pulled five cars, so it only took about thirty seconds to clear the intersection.

One day, the large slab of concrete that bridged the blacktop and the rail became dislodged by heavy truck traffic. The slab angled upward into the road. The city quickly jumped to action, coned off the area, and removed the offending concrete. With the slab of concrete removed, there was a huge hole in the northbound lane. So the city arranged the cones to make the center turn lane the new northbound lane.

Given its proximity to our warehouse, truck drivers heading southbound could no longer use the center lane to make the wide turn needed to enter our property. Due to the rerouted lanes, and because the road had such heavy truck traffic all day, the potential for accidents went way up. Trucks with long loads and wide loads turned in and out of our warehouse. There were bad drivers, confused drivers, and thousands of vehicles flowing through the area. All this regularly destroyed the carefully arranged cones and barriers. I should have started a business selling safety cones and barrels to the city government. I could have retired.

Did the city act quickly to repair the broken slab of concrete? No. After a week, the city sent its crew to reset the cones and barrels. The next week they had to place new ones and to cart away the destroyed ones. After two months of this, Chester started making calls to the city. They referred him to the railroad. The railroad referred him to the port authority. The person at the port said, "We've been meeting with the railroad and the city trying to resolve it. We should have it fixed shortly."

More months went by. Chester followed up with the port, the city, and the railroad. He got nowhere. We watched near miss accidents repeatedly. Trucks battled with other trucks and cars to pass through that narrow stretch of road. The city continued to replace the candlesticks and barrels, but they never fixed the road.

Chester tried calling the local newspaper to see if they would be interested in a story about government inefficiency. The newspaper was not interested. No one seemed to care—until a serious accident occurred. It took three years for someone to take responsibility for a five-by-five hole in a road with heavy traffic that was vital to the port. The city probably spent one hundred times more than the cost of the repair.

One positive thing I can say about government: If you have some of the government's business, you can count on getting paid.

Government Business

Before I started Joel's Warehouse, I had managed my company's contracts and relationships with US Transportation Command (US TRANSCOM), which is the military entity that coordinates supplies for complex missions. Other than that, I have limited exposure to building a business relationship with any level of government.

Many companies exist solely to provide services to the

government. I can understand why. A government is a stable customer. They pay bills on time. The contracts, which are hundreds of pages long, can generate tens of millions of dollars.

At Joel's Warehouse I often tried to find a niche where we could provide services to some level of government, but I never made any headway. We could have become a bonded warehouse and provided customs services, but we never had the time or room in the warehouse to make that work. I scoured the federal business opportunities website, and the state and local government business pages, to find something to bid on. To even *look* at the federal listings, I had to obtain a CAGE code. I think the government wanted to make sure that I was not a Chinese spy or Russian intelligence bot.

I discovered that FEMA might need us to let them use our warehouse in a disaster. Our warehouse was full, so to accommodate FEMA we would have had to wipe out our existing business relationships. Plus, I needed ongoing business, not just in times of crisis.

Maybe it was a good thing that I never landed a government contract. That would have created new reporting and oversight burdens. If a government representative didn't like the reports for any reason, he or she could tell me to fix them or lose the contract. The government would have had more control over how I ran my business, including by setting limits on how much I could charge them. If they caught me charging the government more than a different customer, they could slap me with a penalty.

As a startup owner, you should expect the government to

be . . . well . . . up in your business. If the government passes a law related to vital aspects of your business, you can be sure they will force you to pay for a permit.

14

Marketing

To run a successful startup, you'll obviously need to get your brand out there and attract customers. The challenge with marketing and sales is that any sort of marketing could be a waste of money. What are your capabilities? Who is your target customer? Will you attract more customers by advertising in a local trade magazine or should you throw stickers on bathroom walls of local bars? Does your name convey the right image?

Hopefully, you have carefully considered the name before starting your company.

Name

Joel's Warehouse. The name was simple. It instantly conveyed what our company did. We provided other services also, such as transloading, freight forwarding, and container sales, but most people in our industry knew that warehouses provided a class of services. So, a simple name was an effective way to let potential clients know what we could do.

We rejected many other name variations because they

weren't accurate. We were not Joel's Cold Storage Warehouse, which would have attracted a vastly different clientele. We weren't Joel's Brokerage because we could not arrange freight shipping to and from foreign countries. We weren't Joel's Heavy Lift, or Joel's Long-Haul Trucking. We often worked with those types of companies, but I didn't want to encourage a bunch of calls for services that I would broker to other providers.

It made sense to use Joel's Warehouse. It was simple and stated the nature of our business. We had a warehouse and forklifts, and we performed work with them. That was the image we wanted to convey to customers. When people called us for quotes, they frequently got Joel on the line, the guy who could answer their questions. If they didn't talk to me, they ended up with Chester, who knew more about the operation than I did.

If you see a business name such as Allenny's Pub or Ryan's Fish Tacos, it's clear that someone chose a simple name that clearly communicates to potential customers what the business offers.

You might prefer a more expansive name. Consider a name such as CougGear: Clothing for Women on the Hunt. Or perhaps Peacock: The Store for Young Single Men. Such names are long, but the target audiences have been clearly defined. As a consumer, I appreciate that the messaging leaves no room for confusion, unlike Google. I can immediately conclude that I need not spend money in either place.

Capabilities

As I said before, it is important to know your capabilities—the services you will provide to customers. When you know that, you can tailor your marketing to the customers you want to reach.

The largest exporters in our state were involved with farm produce. We contacted many of these companies to see what services they needed. We discovered that they only needed trucking help. They packed the containers at their farms by themselves. They just needed a steady stream of trucks with empty containers coming from the ports to the fields, and full containers going back to the ports.

Some farmers had large operations with their own trucking fleets. They only needed supplemental trucking during peak seasons. Others had in-house ocean brokers who handled the paperwork and relations with shipping lines. Others used third party brokerages, which again was not a service in our wheelhouse. All said, we could not provide any service to these exporters without changing our identity and focusing more on trucking.

Once we had acquired the lumber transload business, we were able to expand our customer base. That's because all exporters had similar needs for lumber storage and container packing. This was good business until tariff troubles caused lumber exports to crash. When that occurred, we abandoned most of that business.

We discovered that we were good at unloading hand-stacked containers, and palletizing and shrink-wrapping freight. After the lumber business dried up, we turned our focus to these services and found ourselves handling dozens of containers per week.

However, on this side of the pond, distribution centers (DCs) wanted freight to be neatly palletized so that it could be quickly routed on trucks to various places around the country and stored on the DCs' rack systems. Depending on the product, there might be hundreds or thousands of boxes in a container. It all had to be unpacked, counted, palletized, shrink-wrapped, and routed by hand.

When we discovered our talent and warehouse capacity for this sort of work, we chased after more. We eventually landed a contract to deliver pallets to the DCs of some little company called Amazon. Imagine: Joel's Warehouse was delivering thousands of pallets of freight to one the largest companies in the world. It was amazing.

But how did we get our customers' attention to begin with?

Just Keep Talking

I joined several local trucking and freight industry clubs. In addition to holding regular education sessions with local lawmakers and business movers and shakers, the clubs provided a big networking opportunity, specifically the club directories that were sent out annually to the members. Anyone looking for business could mine these directories. I would scour them to find competitors and customers with whom I could build relationships.

Chester and I talked to many people. They would often recommend other prospects. Then we would talk more. We gave out business cards that listed our capabilities at Joel's Warehouse: storage, transloading, freight forwarding, and container sales (ugh). We called, emailed, and followed up with those we had contacted earlier. We also talked to existing customers to see if they knew anyone who would benefit from our services.

The key is that we knew our capabilities. As a result, if a person asked for something outside our wheelhouse, we knew exactly what to say. We saved everyone a lot of time while also quickly building our identity in the market. We earned a strong reputation and lots of business opportunities by being clear and frank. Word-of-mouth marketing generated a lot of business.

As our reputation grew, locally and among a wide array of brokerages, the goodwill followed us for years. It has been years since we stopped operating, but I still field calls for people looking for a recommendation. It is important for me to keep burnishing our reputation.

Advertising

I'm not a marketing guru, but any startup needs to identify the customers and get their attention. That is a basic concept.

I worked for a company that, years after I left, decided to advertise their services on local billboards. I don't know why they considered that to be a good idea because they were in a specialty market. More than 99 percent of the customers who needed their services already knew about the company. Billboard marketing seemed like a waste of money to me. After a few months (maybe a year), the billboard advertisements came down.

My former employer was also engaged with some of the industry clubs to which I belonged. The company frequently advertised in annual directories. Although the ads probably didn't generate new business for my former company, I could understand the rationale for advertising in those publications. First, buying ads supported the clubs and the associated charities. Second, the company's competitors had ads in the club publications, so they needed to follow suit. Third, the ads showed the company logo, which helped the company to stay "top of mind" among customers. These are all good reasons for you to spend on advertising, even when it might not bring in new business.

Joel's warehouse didn't spend much money on advertising. Our business grew by word-of-mouth referrals from existing customers or competitors. We mostly kept talking about ourselves to everyone we met. However, we did allow ourselves to enjoy one vain, glorious moment.

It happened at a charity golf tournament sponsored by a freight club. The money raised at the tournament was used to support a charity. Our company was doing so well that it seemed like we should sponsor a team and buy some advertising.

I had Chester go to the tournament while I stayed and supervised the warehouse. Chester invited three of our customers to be on his team. At the beginning of the course there was a giant banner with the logos of all the sponsors, sorted by contribution level.

My former employer's competitor headlined the banner as the platinum sponsor. Below them, on the gold sponsor tier, was my former employer's logo. Right next to that was the logo of the other gold sponsor: Joel's Warehouse. I took a lot of pleasure in that moment. It was like pitting Mike Tyson during his prime boxing years against a cardboard cutout of the Philadelphia Phillies' Phanatic mascot. We did not deserve to be in the ring against a multibillion-dollar company.

Chester took a picture of the banner. It is a good memory in the history of Joel's Warehouse. We did not get any new business from the advertisement, but we did generate additional business from the customers with whom Chester played golf.

The most important aspect of advertising is to target the right audience, otherwise advertising is a waste of money. That seems simple, but in my experience, people often forget simple truths. Why else would my former company put ads on local billboards?

In my opinion, the best and cheapest route to brand a business is online.

Online Presence

I can think of many reasons to have an online presence. When people need information about a business, such as contact info, the first place they will look is online. People, I think, are naturally curious. They will check out the company website, Facebook page, and Google listing to see if it is legitimate and to evaluate the company's professional image.

I started with a website. I posted basic information, such as our address, contact information, pictures of our space and equipment, and a quote form. I also provided regular updates about our holiday closure schedule. That's about all I did. Most people, in my opinion, look at business websites to find basic information and to ensure that the business is active.

I also made sure to have a Google listing. Long-haul truck drivers often used Google to find directions to the warehouse, which spared me from having to take calls from truck drivers in the middle of the night. Having a Google presence also lent some credibility to our company. People who looked us up got an informative hit.

I also set up a Facebook page, but I did not populate it with much information other than our company name and address. Had we been in a different industry, such as a restaurant, I would have placed more information on that platform. Most of our interactions were business-to-business and done by appointment, so I didn't see a need to provide much detail on Facebook. We also listed ourselves on the local port website. This posting included a general description of our services.

While building our online presence, I tried to put myself in the shoes of our customers, vendors, and others (over-the-road truckers). I imagined the many ways that they might attempt to find Joel's Warehouse or the services that we offered. I could have done more, but no one needed tweets from Joel's Warehouse. We weren't trying to go viral for our superb forklift handling, so we didn't post videos on YouTube or TikTok.

The point is that you need to figure out how your customers will want to interact with you. Then focus your efforts on how to best serve them online. A company with a sloppy online presence is harder to sell. If a customer can't tell when the business is open, or can't find the address, he or she won't come in. A restaurant without an online menu will get fewer customers. People just need the basics that allow them to do business easily.

The most important information should be on the site's landing page. You don't want to bury what your customers most need on the "About" page. People don't need to read about your love of old video games or how Aunt Mildred forked over money so that you could start an arcade with a 1980s theme. People don't need to know that your "twist" is to sell beer to people like me who are old enough to drink beer and old enough to have dropped hundreds of quarters into arcade games in the 1980s. People need to know your hours, that you are a legitimate arcade, and that you serve beer. After that, a few people might click on the "About" link to learn about Aunt Mildred.

15

IT

To run any sort of business today, it will be necessary to understand something about technology. I cannot imagine a business that can survive without it. This is, after all, the modern world.

What You Need

Each type of business needs a customized approach to IT. A gas station operating under a big corporation like Shell might have all the technology mapped out. The franchise owner just needs to connect to the corporate operating systems. The corporation will likely provide documentation and training for everything needed to run the business.

If you're not franchising, the owner must figure out the IT thing on his or her own or hire someone to do it. I never had money to burn, so I did everything I could on my own. What did we need at Joel's Warehouse? A few computers. Katie had her own laptop that she brought from home. The rest of our employees were forklift operators or lumpers who didn't need a computer.

For phone service, we decided to use our cell phones because we didn't have the ability to staff office phones full time. Most cell phone plans offered unlimited minutes, and I spent hours every day in the warehouse. A cell phone allowed me to take calls outside the office. My cell phone also allowed me to take calls from truckers at 2 a.m.

We needed a website, email, printers, a central cloud location for file storage, and software licenses. We needed to run our back office, keep track of freight, and share information with customers. We needed billing, quoting, and accounting systems, and a way to handle payroll.

That was a lot. I was not an IT expert, but I did not want to spend money to hire someone. What follows is how I set up Joel's Warehouse.

Website and Email

I'm a nerd, but not the IT variety. I grew up in a rapidly changing world. In high school, I learned how to type using a typewriter, but the world changed so fast that I never used a typewriter again. Technology keeps changing, so I keep adapting. At some point, I suspect that tech will outpace my ability to adapt.

One of my high school experiments with technology occurred when a friend and I spent months trying to connect a computer running Windows 3.1 to the school's telescope so that the astronomy class could take pictures of the heavens. I was more familiar with computers than my friend. When we succeeded in getting everything to work (against all odds), a parade of school administrators came through the observatory to gawk at the pictures we produced.

In retrospect, it was sort of absurd. The high school had a computer lab with students and a teacher who knew something about computers. Nevertheless, the science teacher responsible for the observatory, who probably hated me, stuck me on the project with a guy I didn't know. The teacher probably hated him too.

The upside is that the experience taught me, at an early age, to cobble together technology and make it work. When we started up Joel's Warehouse, I decided to build the website myself. I knew I could easily do it because, years before, I had already created a video game website just for fun. At the warehouse, I got the job done without hiring someone. That should give you hope. You can set it up yourself.

I used a website hosting company with an easy-to-use interface with drag and drop formatting. I just had to upload pictures of the business and do a little typing. Honestly, doing vertical lookup equations in spreadsheet software is harder than creating a website.

Once we had the website going, the hosting service set up email addresses that exchanged through the domain. This gave us branded email addresses with @joelswarehouse rather than a generic address, which looked much more professional. Setting up the email accounts on our phones and computers was also a cinch.

The credit for making all of this so easy belongs to the smart nerds who design this stuff for average users like me.

They helped me make my company look professional. The cost was a couple of hundred dollars per year and some time. To have a professional handle this would have cost thousands, probably, plus ongoing tech support. I preferred to use that money for something else, like paying for dates with Katie.

After we set up the email, cell phones, and other basic technology, we next needed an operating system. The Holy Grail of operating systems is one that incorporates everything your business does (quotes, operations, rating, billing, AP, AR, HR, finances, sales) in one place. To find this mythical beast, we needed to do research.

Research

Before I made any decisions, I always did some internet research. Whatever the problem, especially IT problems, a solution could be found on the internet. I am a skeptic, so I would read at least three sources, along with customer reviews, to make sure I had seen the best options.

I also asked my competitors about which operating system they used. Some would not tell me, and others said they used a proprietary system. Eventually I would find a competitor who was willing to talk. Such a person often would not shut up until he had told me the pros and cons of every system that exists in the entire market, and that he had just looked at them all last year, and, by the way, here is the business card of the guy who sold the system, and that his employees love the system so much, and would change one thing but it is kind of expensive, but that he still knows it's the best, and he knows he got a better deal than anyone else because he talked with the sales rep and got him to knock some money off, and the sales rep told him he's a great negotiator . . . Then this competitor would abruptly change the conversation to talk about the fishing trip he took last month, and you will start wondering how to end the conversation before you starve to death because it seems like this guy won't shut up. My advice: Write down the systems he mentions and do more internet research.

Third, don't be afraid to demo systems. In most cases, you can try them online. Others might require a face-to-face visit with a sales rep.

After completing the research, we needed to make a decision.

The Back-Office System

I've never seen a back-office system that can do it all. I've been stuck on several teams that tried to implement perfect back-office solutions. They promptly had to figure out workarounds to accommodate all the things the original back-office system couldn't do. Then upper management got mad because they had spent a lot of money on a back-office system that needed workarounds to function. The IT staff then blamed the users for not providing enough information during the research phase, and the users blamed IT for not listening to their needs, and years later everyone remained angry at each other.

I think my bosses appointed me to those teams as a punishment. Either I was too good at my job—what the IT guys called a "super user" who would try things the system was not designed for—or because they wanted me out of the productive flow. Whatever the case, the fact remains that I was an unwilling participant in several implementations.

I learned about implementing back-office systems (BOS) designed to integrate all company activities. I learned that it is easy to get bogged down in intricate details while pursuing the "perfect" system. For example, let's say a system does not provide an entry point for information about one important key performance indicator (KPI). The staff has several options when deciding whether to choose the system or not.

1. Eliminate the system from the list of options
2. Pay for custom enhancements to track the KPI
3. Have an employee manually track the KPI outside the system and report on it
4. Stop tracking the KPI

Option one ends up eliminating all back-office options because no systems will be perfect right out of the gate. Option two, paying for upgrades, is the most popular in my experience. Unfortunately, it ends up being a game that never ends. The new BOS will be rolled out after a ton of modifications, and then users will request new modifications. The company will spend tens of thousands per year on developers who enhance and customize the BOS. Then new management will form a team to implement a different BOS and replace the old one that had been modified for years. And then the new BOS will be heavily modified.

Option three, having an employee manually track the info, is usually the most distasteful to upper management. They do not wish to spend tens of thousands on a new back-office system while also paying an analyst to track information on a spreadsheet few people have access to. Also, in theory, information that is manipulated outside the system is worthless because it lacks the system's validation.

Option four, to stop tracking the KPI, has never been a popular choice. I've never seen anyone successfully get rid of a KPI in a corporate setting. It's much easier to get additional KPIs added than it is to eliminate one. Upper management loves the adrenaline rush that comes from having more ways to measure productivity in relation to the number of bathroom breaks. But dealing with more KPIs is not so great for the operational chump who has a spreadsheet to maintain and weekly reporting requirements.

For these reasons, most of us resort to option 1 and supplement it with option 3. We use an imperfect system and handle the shortfalls manually. Even upper management ends up accepting this option when they realize they have no choice.

At Joel's warehouse the closest we had to a back-office system was QuickBooks. We could not use that program for many functions related to our physical operations. But we were able to use it for quoting, invoicing, payroll, credit card payment receiving, and accrual accounting. Our bank accounts connected to it, so we were able to see our balances in real time. And we could track the checks we had written in relation to the direct deposits we expected to receive. For other needs, I used the two-spreadsheet system I described earlier in the book.

We also used external programs for our operational work. We used Excel to handle bills of lading and other standard forms and we used Word for formal contract documents. We tracked our freight in the warehouse with spreadsheets. One spreadsheet showed the layout of the warehouse and our storage locations by container number or customer reference number. I kept additional spreadsheet tabs for each customer, tracking the inventory as we received it or loaded it out. All of this was backed up with the paper copies of bills of lading.

The system worked well, in part because I was the only person who updated the key spreadsheets. Had our company grown more than it did, we would have needed a warehouse management system for tracking freight.

The point is to choose what will work best for each type of business. By keeping the pros and cons I've discussed in mind, you can reduce stress and save money. Otherwise, hire a knowledgeable IT person.

When choosing our IT system, we also had to keep the customers in mind.

Customers and IT Decisions

Customers can be a huge factor in IT choices. We kept track of our freight inventory with a spreadsheet because most of our customers were familiar with them. Our approach might not have worked for Fortune 500 customers who expect EDI transmission between systems. Had we worked with those types of clients, we probably would have made an expensive software purchase. However, in our experience, high-end customers usually have their own web-based systems for their vendors. In this case, a small startup like ours could gain permission to log in to the customer's system to enter that data, which would be cheaper than investing in software.

If you are trying to land a big customer, they will want to know how to interact with you. Feel free to ask if they have a vendor solution that you can use instead of investing in your own.

16

Work-Life Balance

Here's a topic that's gained steam in recent decades: work-life balance.

We all know what it means. It's code for, "I'm working too many hours and have too little life." We never hear the opposite: "I have too much free time and not enough time at work."

It doesn't help that cell phones and laptops can tether you to your work no matter where you are. A ringing phone is almost impossible to ignore, especially when a missed call could be a missed opportunity.

The good and the bad of owning a startup is that the owner gets more say over how much work gets done each day. However, time does not belong to the owner. He or she must consider the needs of customers.

Customers Own You

Without customers, the job would be easy. Wear and tear on forklifts would be minimal. There wouldn't be much paperwork to shuffle. We could drink coffee all day, gossip with coworkers, flirt with the cute vendor, and go home.

Business owners owe their time to the people who pay them: the customers. To a certain extent, *they* are the bosses. To be successful, the startup owner must work the hours that customers need. A coffee shop owner must be willing to open early in the morning. An owner of a restaurant and bar should be prepared to stay open until 2 a.m. To run a fast-food restaurant someone must work around the clock, seven days a week. Good managers and other staff can ease the owner's load, but the owner will be on the hook for most of the hours, especially as the business is getting started.

During the owner's "free time," he or she will be thinking about the business because an entire life savings is sunk into the venture. It *must* succeed.

The key to at least *trying* to find a work-life balance is to understand what the customers will require from the business and then to figure out personal limitations and capacity. I once thought it would be fun to own a bar. Unfortunately, I can't stay up past 10 p.m. these days because I'm getting old. A bar would not be a good match for me, especially given my personality and desire to be deeply involved in an operation.

My maternal grandparents owned a little mercantile for more than twenty years. The business was open seven days a week. As far as I can remember, they only closed the store on Christmas. My grandmother got up early and opened the store at six every morning. My grandfather started later so that he could close the store at nine at night. They took two or three vacations while I was growing up. They couldn't, or wouldn't, trust the store to other people for extended periods of time. They were at the store day in and day out until they retired and sold it. They did have a great retirement in compensation for all the years of hard work.

I don't think most people could handle that type of commitment. But my grandparents understood that they had to do what was necessary to provide what the customers needed.

Our customer, Little Jimmy, could be demanding at times. His customers demanded a lot from him, and he tried to juggle his drivers to get more done each day. At times, he wanted us to start work at five in the morning and stay until six at night. Sometimes we accommodated him, and sometimes we proposed better alternatives, such as working on a Saturday morning. Sometimes we had other work to prioritize, which affected whether we could say yes or no to his requests. After all, he had hired us because we offered more flexibility than other warehouses.

Little Jimmy was also struggling to find a good work-life balance. His efforts to generate revenue created problems that were understandable, but sometimes he asked too much of his workers, such as asking them to work ten or twelve hours a day for six days a week. In such a case, a driver or two would quit.

As we got busier, our struggle to balance work and life got worse. Ultimately, we decided to "make hay while the sun shined." During our third summer in business, I worked ten out of the twelve Saturdays. That's how busy we were. On those Saturdays, we would call a dozen lumpers to help us pound through all the containers that we had not handled the prior week. The lumpers would sort through thousands of boxes, palletize the product, and get everything stored in nice rows. We would also do a couple of bulk loadouts for Little Jimmy, which allowed us to get a head start on the following week.

Even on my fortieth birthday, a Saturday, I worked. Katie threw me a big party, which I was only slightly late for. There was not much life those years, but I was making hay while the sun shined.

I have developed some strategies to compensate for years of overwork.

Balance

During my years of running Joel's Warehouse, both of my kids were young. The oldest went to school near the route I took to and from work. By the third year of the business, my youngest son had joined him at the same school. Fortunately, the school had after-hours care, so on most days I picked them up after work. That gave me opportunities to take them places before we went home, such as to play miniature golf. I took them to karate class and other activities, at least once or twice per week. Katie sometimes came with me to work in the office while the boys watched movies in the warehouse.

I could have used work as an excuse to avoid these responsibilities. Between Katie and my mother-in-law, the kids could have been cared for without me. That would have left me more time to focus on the business. But the question I asked myself was: why?

I sometimes wonder what might have happened if I had thrown more time and energy into the business. I could have worked on Sundays too, or showed up at the warehouse at 6 a.m. instead of 7 a.m. I could have left work at 8 p.m. instead of at 4 p.m. For that matter, I could have put a shower in the warehouse bathroom and a pull-out sofa in the office.

Perhaps by giving myself completely to work, we could have opened ten warehouses spread across three states. Alongside the warehouse operations, we could have managed a fleet of one hundred trucks. Maybe I could have employed hundreds of employees and generated tens of millions in sales. I could have bought Chester out of the company, sent him into retirement with a golden parachute, and built my own pyramid of gold.

Perhaps.

Had I made that sacrifice, there would have been a definite loss; I would have lost the privilege of raising my children. My *reason* for working was to provide for the kids. Katie and I made a commitment to raise them. That commitment meant, to me, that I needed to be involved with the family. If the business was providing a living, which it was, then I did not need to sacrifice more of my time.

You, as the business owner, need to ask that same question. If you're earning a decent living, do you want to give up time for more money?

I was forced to do some soul searching when my father-in-law passed away at age sixty-three from cancer. He was extremely successful in business. He spent his later years traveling for work at least six months out of the year. He was on a plane every other week. A family friend once observed that my father-in-law had "a schedule that could kill a horse." With grown children, he was able to take most of these trips with my mother-in-law. It was good that they had this time together.

Unfortunately, my father-in-law never saw retirement. He had big plans about road tripping through Europe. He saw his daughters get married, but he never met any of his grandkids. It wasn't fair. Life seldom is.

That story provided me with some perspective. I decided that I did not want to live to work. I decided to work to live.

I have known people who refuse to retire, even at age seventy or older, even though they have sufficient money and benefits. Their companies forced them into retirement. Why won't they give it up?

Many politicians, including those in primary positions of power, are in their seventies and eighties. These folks should be spending time in Arizona and Florida in the winter and visiting their families and grandkids during the summer. They should be taking vacations to Europe or Asia (or elsewhere). Why are they spending their twilight years flying back and forth to Washington, DC to engage in angry political battles? Perhaps it's an attraction to power. Perhaps they would lack purpose in life if they retired. Maybe they don't realize how little time they have left. My father-in-law's story is a reminder that a cancer diagnosis can put a literal deadline on our lives here.

I'm not a procrastinator. If something is worth doing, it

is worth doing today. That includes spending time with my family. I will never get missed time with them back. If I did not have that perspective, it would be easy to get wrapped up in my job.

Owning a startup is a lot like having a baby. It's yours and it requires a lot of dedication to raise it. But, in my view, it should not be *the* baby.

The balance between work and life will have to be designed by you. Look for opportunities to leave work early. If eighty-hour weeks become the rule instead of the exception, think about a job change. As Stephen Covey would say, "Begin with the end in mind." Decades from now, you will look back and either have memories of work or memories of life. I know which I'd prefer.

17

Better to Be Lucky

"I'd rather be lucky than good." That was one of Chester's many sayings. It has a kernel of truth, although we hate to admit it. The idea that being lucky is a factor for success is hard to accept. We like to think that determination and grit is sufficient for achievement. We prefer to believe that failure is the result of not working smart enough. We think that failure is only for those who give up.

Unfortunately, hard work is not enough.

Grit Isn't Enough

It obviously takes intelligence and hard work to run a successful company. If a guy tried to sell horse shit sandwiches as a vegan alternative to roast beef, he could work endlessly and still fail. The idea literally stinks. Luck is not a substitute for brains.

But . . . imagine a business that makes widgets for cars. The widgets are in high demand among car manufacturers. The business owner inks two big deals. The idea is great and the sales presentation is spot on. With the deals in place, the owner has six months to get the manufacturing facility up and running.

A year later, everything is humming along except that a crucial component made in China suddenly can't be imported due to a trade war. It will take months before another manufacturer can be found and brought up to speed. The owner considers the possibility of producing it in house, but there's not enough money to invest in the needed machinery. To make matters worse, the auto production line has stopped because the cars require the widget to function. Bills keep piling up.

None of this is the business owner's fault. The business plan was sound, and the customers were happy. So what happened? A stroke of bad luck. Now the future of the business is uncertain. There is no guarantee that working harder will get the company out of the mess.

Or consider a restaurateur whose dream is to start a fusion restaurant that merges American breakfast fare with Indian curry dishes. The business launches and early signs are positive. The location is good, the food is getting good customer feedback, and repeat business is strong.

Unbeknownst to the owner, a local food critic who happens to live down the street decides to try the new restaurant. The next day a positive article about the restaurant appears in the local paper. Business triples overnight. Instead of just doing well, the business owner begins to make more money than she ever dreamed possible. On Fridays there is a two-hour wait to be seated. The restaurant is officially a success.

In both situations, luck played a major role in the outcome.

Unfortunately, business books rarely mention the luck factor. There are, of course, some honest moments when well-known leaders and authors admit that luck helped them. In fact, I know some business leaders who admit that luck has played a role in their success. But I've come to believe that anyone who denies the role of luck in business is either lying or ignorant.

Do not get me wrong; I'm not saying that hard work isn't a requirement for starting and growing a business. However, people who do all the right things can still end up with terrible outcomes. As we all know, life isn't fair.

During the Covid-19 pandemic, unfairness played out as many small businesses, and even large brick and mortar stores permanently closed. As a startup owner myself, one who assumed the normal business risks (competition, market forces, etc.), it is hard to swallow the fact that a stroke of a bureaucrat's pen can destroy a company. I'm not going to spend time arguing for or against the lockdowns that occurred, but many small business owners and employees are now faced with unemployment and possible homelessness through no fault of their own.

Warehouse Luck

A massive stroke of luck enabled me to start Joel's Warehouse. We needed a warehouse to lease. However, most warehouse owners did not want to give a startup the opportunity to lease space. Secondarily, there was a wide discrepancy between the amount of available space and what we needed.

We found some warehouses with ten thousand square feet, but we needed about fifteen thousand square feet for Little Jimmy's product alone. We also found some places with fifty thousand to one hundred thousand square feet. The owners were willing to talk to us, but we couldn't afford the rent on such a large warehouse. Ideally, we would find a warehouse with about thirty thousand square feet. This would be big enough to handle Little Jimmy's freight and to add more customers while being small enough to keep our rent as low as possible.

Our best opportunity was a place where the tenant was moving out and looking for someone to assume a two-year sublease. The warehouse was only twenty thousand square feet, but the warehouse owner was offering a sweetheart price that would make it a safe deal for our startup. However, the owners were extremely reticent to deal with a couple of unknown dudes like Chester and me. Everyone was looking for a blue-chip company with a long history.

We were at least able to start negotiations for the warehouse. The owners requested us to pay two years of the lease *up front*, to the tune of about $180,000. I took a deep breath, went to the bank, and put up the equity in my home. I didn't even ask Chester to put up 40 percent because I knew I would be asking too much.

When I told the warehouse owners that I would accept their terms, they backed out completely and told us they were no longer interested in further discussions. It was a crushing rejection. I was bitter enough to enjoy the fact that they never found another party to sublease the warehouse. They ended up on the hook for the remaining term.

Meanwhile, we had been talking to customers other than Little Jimmy. We wanted to determine whether we could bring in enough business to justify a warehouse with fifty thousand square feet. None of those potential customers seemed ready to commit to working with us. We could not justify the risk.

Things were at a standstill until the realtor and I made a follow-up visit to check out a fifty-thousand-square-foot building where half of the space was available. We arrived at around eight in the morning. By sheer *luck*, the owner of the building, a gentleman from a state two thousand miles away, happened to be there. He had flown in the night before to visit his properties. He planned to fly out later that day.

He was generous enough to give me an hour of his time. We talked about the business I was trying to set up and about Little Jimmy's freight. I tried to show him that I was a good risk, that I would take care of his building and pay my bills. His philosophy in life was like mine. We got along well. He decided to give us a chance.

Joel's Warehouse finally had a home. The realtor and I decided to check it out at the exact moment when the owner was there. The owner only came *twice* a year for short visits. I can only attribute it to luck.

This luck ended up repeating over the years, in a market where finding warehouse space was difficult. Many warehouses were being built every year to keep up with demand. But we were always able to find ways to meet our customers' needs.

Mysterious Loads of Luck

You might remember the story about the Thanksgiving miracle. We had been operating for only nine months when we received the shocking news that Little Jimmy's biggest customer had over one hundred loads arriving soon. This news came when Little Jimmy was in Mexico to celebrate turkey day with a Pina Colada in each hand. Moreover, our warehouse was already completely full.

But there was a lucky silver lining. This situation pushed us to search for more space. Through our realtor, we connected with competitors who gave us a short-term lease. With access to their space, we were able to take on the additional work. The combination of the good relationship and the availability meant we got a temporary warehouse deal done in two days. Acquiring a warehouse in two days during Thanksgiving week was a warehousing miracle.

At the same time, we saw that Little Jimmy's business had been contracting by about 10 percent a year. This seemed bad at first, but it encouraged us to procure business that paid better. As his product dwindled, we had more space to accept higher paying clients. Over the years, Little Jimmy's freight contracted by 40 percent, but our company was doing better than ever.

As another example of luck, we started getting frequent and mysterious loads that would show up unannounced. There were no identifying marks to tell us who was in control of the freight. We could not recognize the shipper. The only party we could recognize was the consignee.

The freight? One time it was tens of thousands of French Bulldog calendars for the following year. Only French Bulldogs! No other breed! We suspected that someone was pranking us. It was absurd (to us).

A couple of days later, we found out that a freight broker we knew had decided to use us but forgot to let us know. The freight was destined for various Amazon distribution centers to be sold for Christmas.

More mysterious loads showed up. There was the load of candy. Then there was the load of soda. Then loads of machinery. That was followed by a load of fire extinguishers. Although we didn't enjoy the surprise loads that kept randomly arriving, it was good to see our business growing. Pure luck.

More good fortune came our way when we learned that one of Little Jimmy's customers might make a massive one-time product purchase, in the range of 130 to 150 containers. Coincidentally, we had just acquired our neighbor's lumber business, which gave us control over all fifty thousand square feet of the warehouse. We had also increased our staff by adding MP and Terry. By rejuggling the existing freight in the warehouse, we were able to clear out part of the lumber side and make room for the huge influx of loads.

As good as everything was going, I was becoming a little worried about the stability of business overall. There were some dark storm clouds on the horizon. Our risk had increased, and I knew that good luck was fickle. I couldn't justify the struggle anymore. As if to confirm my skepticism, the misses began to pile up.

Missed Opportunities

There is such a thing as bad luck.

During our first month of operation, Chester was on a flight and ended up sitting next to a guy who needed to buy more than two hundred containers. His business involved building wilderness camps for oil crews. This was, and maybe still is, a booming business in parts of the country. The crews working in remote oil fields needed showers, beds, and other necessities. Shipping containers function well for some of these purposes.

We were interested in wholesale container sales, and we previously had success in selling containers to people in remote areas. We had the connections to get the containers delivered to remote areas cheaply.

We also needed a win to jump start our business. We were frazzled and stressed by learning how to run our company. Selling containers to this group could have helped our bank accounts, opened us to long-term container sales, and provided some peace of mind after a rocky start.

We reached out to the person Chester met on the plane, but we didn't connect. In the meantime, we made sure that we had all the containers from the vendor. We planned the routes for making the deliveries to the remote camps. We prepared our quote. Then we followed up with the guy again.

He was difficult to get ahold of. I got an email from him that had a computer virus. (I didn't open it.) Chester visited the man's location, where the camp was to be built. After that he was impossible to reach. He never responded to emails or messages. A few months later, I called him out of the blue. He finally admitted that he had bought his containers from someone else.

It was the lack of courtesy that hurt most. He knew we were getting started and needed a big win. After that, our dreams of selling containers faltered. The reseller permit and other business licenses I had acquired ended up being for naught.

After a period of strong growth that enabled us to expand into fifty thousand square feet of warehouse space, a lot of hard things began to happen simultaneously. Chester's health turned for the worse and the lumber business began to shrink due to tariff wars. Could we weather the storm?

For a while it seemed like the answer would be yes. As the supersacks in the warehouse dwindled, we were able to replace them with boxed mattresses. Then, the mattress folks received bad news. The local Amazon distribution center would no longer accept their product due to limitations with the fire suppression system. All future loads would be shipped by rail to an Amazon warehouse two thousand miles away. The mattress customer had no choice but to comply.

With the lumber and the mattresses gone, we could no longer hold on to the entire warehouse. I found someone to pick up the lease on that half of the building and we were back to our original spacc.

We had been on a wild ride, and we still had a few months left on our original three-year agreement for the twenty-five thousand square feet. It was time for some good news.

18

Closure

It is probably apparent by now that Joel's Warehouse is no more. We became just another "failure" statistic. According to a *Forbes* article in 2018, more than 80 percent of businesses survive the first year, but only about half survive for five years. We made it work for three years.

This has led me to do a lot of thinking about failure. I've had friends and family members with "failed" marriages. My company "failed" to last even four years. Many people think this country has "failed" (insert your reason here).

After a lot of soul-searching, I've rejected the broad overuse of the word *failure*. It is applied too liberally. Like many words, it needs context.

Context

The opposite of failure is success. By that strict definition, any company, regardless of its purpose, duration in existence, or the events leading to closure automatically gets labeled as a failure when the doors shut. Companies with a hundred years of success end up being defined by the final day. In that sense, Joel's Warehouse is in good company with Blockbuster, Kodak, Borders, and—a childhood favorite of mine—Toys R Us.

Failure is too strong a word.

In many cases, we could say that companies failed to adapt. That would be a reason why Blockbuster went out of business. But they are not alone. According to the American Enterprise Institute, only sixty of the Fortune 500 companies that existed in 1955 were still Fortune 500 companies in 2017. The failures of companies are replete with stories of mergers, technological changes, and obsolescence.

I don't think it would be a stretch to say that in fifty years there will be a big turnover of companies. Many familiar names will be gone. I doubt that companies like Facebook (now Meta, whatever that means) and Netflix will exist in fifty years. Technology will change. Markets will change. We will look back on those companies and realize they were products of their time. In the future, assuming that our consciousnesses are all linked to the cloud via brain implants, there will be no need for services like Facebook and Netflix; we'll be streaming information all the time directly into our brains.

Should we call businesses that served their times "failures"? Blockbuster was a product of its time. During their twenty-five years in business, Blockbuster completely dominated the home movie rental market. They provided jobs for tens of thousands of people and value for tens of millions of customers. I used to rent movies and video games from them. They were a massive success. Then the world moved on.

Likewise, I have a hard time considering Joel's Warehouse to be a failure. "Lasting into perpetuity" was never a goal. Nothing lasts into perpetuity, not even Fortune 500 companies with seemingly endless resources and tens of thousands of creative thinkers.

Chester and I wanted to be in control of our destinies, to support our families, and to have some fun along the way. We checked off all those boxes at Joel's Warehouse. We worked hard to build the business, but we had other factors to consider.

Chester was the "wise elder" before we started the company. Three years of labor in the warehouse, a health struggle, and the unrelenting march of time did not make him any younger, even though he pretended he would be "eighteen until I die." Our next obligation to the warehouse would have been a five-year term. Chester couldn't commit to that. He would have been eighty at the end of that lease term.

I had options to keep the business going. I could have tried to do it on my own. Little Jimmy wanted to buy Chester's part of the company so that I could keep handling his freight. I could have found a replacement for Chester and kept up the fight. I could have depended on stupendous luck to keep the business moving into the future.

But I knew that the unabashed amount of good luck we had from inception would not last forever. I was afraid that we would hit a bad streak, and that without Chester I would be required to fight alone. Ultimately, I couldn't see myself doing it, not at the great personal cost to me and my family.

The good news was that we had an exit strategy.

Exit Strategy

Chester and I had long relationships with various folks in the transportation industry. We knew one guy who had a big warehouse and not enough business. It seemed like there might be some synergy between us. He needed the business and we needed a way out.

It took a few weeks, but the deal came together. Our colleague bought all our assets (forklifts, dock plates, yard hostler, etc.), hired all our employees, brought Chester on in a consultative sales role, and even offered me a job running the combined business. It couldn't have been a better match for all of us.

The only hitch was that I didn't want the job of running the combined businesses. That turned out to not be a roadblock. When the deal commenced, we moved our existing freight to the other warehouse. I bowed out after making sure that the customers and employees were situated.

Over the next six months, I wrapped up Joel's Warehouse. I had to legally and financially close the corporation and business. I paid the last of the bills and taxes. I collected the rest of the receivables. I dealt with the accountants. I wrote bonus checks to Mutt, Juan Carlos, Katie, and other employees who had supported us through the transition.

Then I gave Chester 40 percent of what was remaining and kept the other 60 percent for myself as per our ownership split. It wasn't enough money for me to retire at the age of forty, but it was enough to prevent me from worrying about my financial stability. That was a good place to be given that the pandemic has caused so much chaos in the business and job market. (Luck found me yet again.)

You can see why I have a hard time defining our closure as a failure. Given the challenges we overcame, the sacrifices we made, and the ultimate positive outcome for everyone involved, I would say that we *survived*.

The Final Word

Months after we had sold the business, I got a call from The Aussie.

"Mate, how are you doing?"

"Good Aussie, how about you?"

"I got some vehicles coming in, wondering if you wanted to give them a shot?"

"We sold the business," I replied. "But Chester is doing sales for a warehouse company that also has a ramp. How about I text his info to you?"

"Congratulations on the sale, mate. Thanks for sending that over. Let me know where you end up!"

"Will do, take care."

Turns out that firing a customer doesn't equate to firing the relationship. However, I knew there was no way in hell that Chester would touch the Aussie's vehicles again.

In the intervening years, I've continued to receive calls from folks looking for Joel's Warehouse. These people usually Google us and realize that I listed the business as closed, but they call anyway hoping that someone can help. I usually direct them to Chester.

Thankfully, my freight-mares have stopped. I don't miss those a bit. It's nice to consistently sleep through the night. I don't miss the late calls from truckers either. I certainly don't miss watching Mutt pee off the dock or watching a Porsche delicately balancing on the end of forklift spears.

On the flip-side, I miss the thrill of seeing a beautiful forty-thousand-pound load of crates single-stacked in a container. I liked showing up at the warehouse every day to plan the work and work the plan. I miss the camaraderie. I miss driving a forklift. For the most part, our customers loved us and we loved them. I miss taking customers out to the minor league park to catch a ballgame and a few beers. I miss knowing that we were building a business and overcoming challenges.

Regardless of where you are in life, I hope you are enjoying yourself. I hope you feel like you are making a positive difference in your life and the lives of those around you. If you have a passion, I hope you pursue it.

If that passion is starting a new business, give me a call first and let me talk you through it. I will not try to talk you out of it, but I will suggest that you build a plan first and print it out on soft, thin paper. Then, when the plan goes to shit—like they always do—you can use it for emergency toilet paper.

If you adapt, I'm sure you will survive.